MOTOR

FORD

Maintenance & Repair Guide

For 1970-77 Models
Galaxie
LTD
Custom
XL

Editor
Louis C. Forier, SAE

FORD
Maintenance & Repair Guide
Library of Congress
Catalog Number: 77-78162
ISBN 0-910992-79-7

Published by

M O T O R

1790 Broadway, New York, N. Y. 10019

Printed in the U.S.A. © Copyright 1977 by the Hearst Corporation

Table of Contents

COOLING SYSTEM

BRAKES

SUSPENSION

ENGINE

CLUTCH, TRANSMISSION & PROPELLER SHAFT

TROUBLE DIAGNOSIS GUIDE

Introduction to Maintenance

This book will save you money even if you have never before done your own car maintenance and repairs. It will not make you a professional auto mechanic. It will not even make you a ''professional'' do-it-yourselfer. But, by being completely devoted to your *particular car* and by telling you how to care for the important things that require little if any technical skill, this book will help you to save money. Your own motivation is all that is necessary to go along with this handy, simply written, confidence-building guide. And even if you *never* do any of the routine maintenance and easy repairs which we have included, this book may nonetheless still save you money! How? By being packed with hundreds and hundreds of tips and insights about *your* car, this book will increase your ''car savvy''. So when you do entrust your car to a professional auto mechanic, you will do so intelligently, confidently and economically.

In producing this guide, we first, carefully selected only those money-saving items of maintenance and repair that you can surely do yourself even if you are not a do-it-yourselfer. Then we prepared the step-by-step instructions in clear, simply everyday language. Finally, we illustrated all of the important points with scores of ''show-me-how'' drawing and photographs, As a result, you will quickly find yourself becoming familiar with routine maintenance, tune-up and replacement of easily accessible parts. All of the normal maintenance parts that you may need are readily available at mass merchandisers at discount prices. So, with you providing some time and a reasonable amount of effort, you will find that saving money will not only be easily possible, but actually enjoyable.

In using this book only a minimal selection of tools will be needed and you may already own many of these. It is desirable to have access to a set of wrenches (socket, open end and box),a wire gauge, a flat blade type feeler gauge, screwdrivers, channel lock pliers and possibly an inexpensive dwell/tachometer-timing light. A torque wrench will become desirable if you become involved in doing major work. However, in the main, we have avoided the use of special tools. Jacks and lifting devices, where required, can be rented at local rent-all centers.

With this in mind, you can begin saving some of those dollars by acquainting youself with the contents of this valuable guide. You may be surprised at just how quickly you can learn the many ways of saving money by doing your own car maintenance and repairs.

Trust yourself—you can do it.

ENGINE IDENTIFICATION

In order to provide accurate car care, it is absolutely necessary to identify your car properly. We are sure you know the year of your own car but you may not know the year and size of the engine. The chart following lists the various engine code letters in relation to the engine size and year of the engine. The engine code is the last letter in the

Year	Engine	Engine Code
1970	6-240	V
	V8-302①	F
	V8-351 (W)①	H
	V8-390①	Y
	V8-390③	X
	V8-429①	K
	V8-429②	N
1971	6-240	V
	V8-302①	F
	V8-351①	H
	V8-390①	Y
	V8-400①	S
	V8-429①	K
	V8-429①	N
1972	6-240	V
	V8-302①	F
	V8-351①	H
	V8-351④	Q
	V8-400	S
	V8-429	N
1973	V8-351	H
	V8-400	S
	V8-429	N
	V8-460	A
1974-77	V8-351	H
	V8-400	S
	V8-460	A

①—Two barrel carburetor.
②—Four barrel carburetor.
③—Premium fuel.
④—Four barrel special.

serial number on the vehicle warranty plate.

MAINTENANCE

To acquaint you with the easiest kinds of maintenance first, we have in-cluded here the factory recommended lubrication and maintenance lists and charts. These lists contain the various mileage intervals at which certain car services are necessary. Good car care habits are important to long car life. A small investment of your time here will pay off many times over in the long term. Many problems experienced by car owners are directly caused by a lack of proper maintenance. A drop off in engine performance or fuel mileage can be caused by a dirty air filter. Hard starting may be traceable to spark plugs with badly worn electrodes, due to their not being replaced at proper intervals. Engine noises are many times caused by the fact that the engine oil has not been changed in ages. Clean oil and filters are perhaps the cheapest items in good car care.

Start now to keep track of your car's needs. A few hours a month devoted to your car care can save you many dollars and keep your car running in top form. And a car in good tune uses less fuel.

CHANGING YOUR ENGINE OIL & OIL FILTER

The best time to change the engine oil is after the engine has been running for a while. This allows the oil to drain more quickly and helps to remove any sludge that may have accumulated in the oil pan. The oil pan drain plug is located in the large bulge at the bottom of the oil pan.

Use a large plastic pan capable of holding about 6 quarts. Place the pan under the drain plug and remove the drain plug. An adjustable wrench can

1970 MAINTENANCE SCHEDULE

Maintenance Operation	Service Interval					
Number of months or thousands of miles, whichever comes first	6	12	18	24	30	36
Change Oil and Filter	X	X	X	X	X	X
Check transmission oil level	X	X	X	X	X	X
Check rear axle fluid level	X	X	X	X	X	X
Check power steering reservoir fluid level	X	X	X	X	X	X
Check brake master cylinder fluid level	X	X	X	X	X	X
Clean crankcase oil filler breather cap	X	X	X	X	X	X
Lube steering linkage						X
Lube front suspension ball joints						X
Check steering linkage joints for abnormal looseness or damaged seals.		X		X		X
Check exhaust control valve for free operation	X	X	X	X	X	X
Replace fuel system filler and check fuel line connections for leaks		X		X		X
Replace carburetor air cleaner filter—6 Cyl. only		X		X		X
Replace carburetor air cleaner filter—8 Cyl. only				X		
Inspect & clean (as necessary) crankcase breather element (in air cleaner) if so equipped.	X	X	X	X	X	X
Replace crankcase emission system, hoses, tubes, fittings, carburetor spacer, oil separator assembly, and replace as necessary. Replace emission control valve		X		X		X
Check and adjust distributor points—replace as required		X		X		X
Check and adjust ignition timing—initial timing, mechanical and vacuum advances, and vacuum retard (if so equipped)		X		X		X
Inspect ignition wiring (Secondary) for proper installation and good condition		X		X		X
Inspect, clean, adjust and test spark plugs—replace as required		X		X		X
Check drive belts for tension and wear. Adjust or replace as required.		X		X		X
Inspect cooling system hoses for deterioration, leaks and loose hose clamps. Repair and/or replace as necessary.		X		X		X
Drain and flush cooling system, replace coolant				Every 24 Months		
Clean and repack front wheel bearings				X		
Check brake lines and lining				X		
Check clutch pedal free play—Adjust linkage if required	X	X	X	X	X	X
Replace fuel evaporative emission control valve (Vehicles built for Calif. registration)		X		X		X

1971 MAINTENANCE SCHEDULE

Maintenance Operation	Service Interval					
Number of months or thousands of miles, whichever comes first	6	12	18	24	30	36
Check brake lines and lining					X	
Check exhaust control valve for free operation (if so equipped)	X	X	X	X	X	X
Inspect cooling system hoses for deterioration, leaks and loose hose clamps. Repair and/or replace as necessary.		X		X		X
Drain and flush cooling system, replace coolant	Every 24 Months					
Replace crankcase breather element (in air cleaner)	X	X	X	X	X	X
Replace fuel system filter and check fuel line connections for leaks		X		X		X
Replace carburetor air cleaner filter—6 Cyl. only		X		X		X
Replace carburetor air cleaner filter—8 Cyl. only				X		
Clean crankcase emission system, hoses, tubes, fittings, carburetor spacer (oil separator assembly, 390 engine only) and replace as necessary. Replace emission control valve.		X		X		X
Check and adjust distributor points—replace as required		X		X		X
Check and adjust ignition timing—initial timing, mechanical and vacuum advances, and vacuum retard (if so equipped)		X		X		X
Inspect ignition wiring (Secondary) for proper installation and good condition		X		X		X
Inspect, clean, adjust and test spark plugs—replace as required		X		X		X
Check drive belts for tension and wear. Adjust or replace as required.		X		X		X
Check clutch pedal free play—Adjust linkage if required	X	X	X	X	X	X
Clean and repack front wheel bearings					X	
Change Oil and Filter	X	X	X	X	X	X
Check transmission oil level	X	X	X	X	X	X
Check power steering reservoir fluid level	X	X	X	X	X	X
Check brake master cylinder fluid level	X	X	X	X	X	X
Lube steering linkage						X
Lube front suspension ball joints						X
Check rear axle fluid level	X	X	X	X	X	X

be used in most cases to remove the plug but in other cases a recessed head may be found on the drain plug which necessitates the use of a tool made for this plug. Auto parts stores carry this tool and it is inexpensive compared to the money you can save by changing your own oil and filter. Allow the oil to drain into the pan and then replace the plug. Screw it in a few turns with your fingers to make sure it is not cross-threaded. Tighten the plug. *If you*

1972 MAINTENANCE SCHEDULE

Maintenance Operation	Service Interval					
Number of months or thousands of miles, whichever comes first	6	12	18	24	30	36
Change engine oil and oil filter	X	X	X	X	X	X
Replace carburetor air cleaner element		X		X		X
Replace fuel filter, check lines for leaks		X		X		X
Replace crankcase emission filter in air cleaner	X	X	X	X	X	X
Clean crankcase oil filler breather cap, if so equipped	X	X	X	X	X	X
Replace PCV valve. Clean emission hoses, tubes.		X		X		X
Replace evaporative emission canister and purge hose				X		
Replace distributor points and condenser		X		X		X
Replace spark plugs		X		X		X
Replace distributor cap and rotor				X		
Check and adjust ignition timing		X		X		X
Inspect cooling system coolant. Check belts		X		X		X
Drain and flush cooling system				X		
Inspect brake lining. Clean and repack front wheel bearings					X	
Check clutch pedal free play. Adjust if required	X	X	X	X	X	X
Check rear axle fluid level	X	X	X	X	X	X
Check transmission fluid level	X	X	X	X	X	X
Check brake master cylinder fluid level	X	X	X	X	X	X
Lubricate front suspension ball joints and steering linkage						X

should crossthread the plug and strip the threads, don't worry, the parts stores carry replacement plugs made just for this reason. Next, using an oil filter strap wrench, unscrew the oil filter. The filter is found on the side of the engine block and it resembles a large can with fluted edges so you can grip it with your hand. As you un-screw the filter, keep it over the drain pan as it contains oil. Pour the oil out of it and dispose of the old filter in the box the new one came in. Next, smear a little oil on the rubber seal at the bottom of the new oil filter, Fig. 1,

Fig. 1   Installing oil filter

1973 MAINTENANCE SCHEDULE (continued)

MAINTENANCE INTERVALS
MILEAGE IN THOUSANDS, OR TIME IN MONTHS, WHICHEVER OCCURS FIRST

	4	8	12	16	20	24	28	32	36
Coolant Condition & Protection			Check			Replace			Check
Cooling System Hoses & Clamps			Check			Check			Check
All Drive Belts			Check			Check			Check
Distributor Cap & Rotor						Inspect			Inspect
Evaporative Emission Canister						Inspect			
Power Steering Fluid Level		Check	Check	Check	Check	Check	Check	Check	Check
Rear Axle Fluid Level			Check	Check	Check	Check	Check	Check	Check
Automatic Transmission Fluid Level			Check	Check	Check	Check	Check	Check	Check
Manual Transmission Fluid Level			Check	Check	Check	Check	Check	Check	Check
Brake Master Cylinder Fluid Level			Check	Check	Check	Check	Check	Check	Check
Clutch Pedal Free Play			Adjust		Adjust		Adjust		Adjust
Clutch and Transmission Linkage			Check			Check			Check
Front Wheel Bearings						Clean & Repack			
Brake Lines and Lining						Inspect			
Front Suspension, Ball Joints									Lubricate
Steering Linkage									Lubricate

1973 MAINTENANCE SCHEDULE

MAINTENANCE INTERVALS
MILEAGE IN THOUSANDS, OR TIME IN MONTHS, WHICHEVER OCCURS FIRST

	4	8	12	16	20	24	28	32	36
Engine Oil	Change	Change	Change	Change	Change	Change	Change	Change	Change
Engine Oil Filter	Replace		Replace		Replace		Replace		Replace
Crankcase-Emission Filter in Air Cleaner			Replace		Replace		Replace		Replace
Carburetor Air Cleaner Element				Replace		Replace		Replace	
Exhaust Control Valve		Lubricate & Free-up		Lubricate & Free-up		Lubricate & Free-up		Lubricate & Free-up	
Crankcase Breather Cap			Clean			Clean			Clean
Spark Plugs			Replace			Replace			Replace
Initial Ignition Timing			Adjust			Adjust			Adjust
Distributor Points			Inspect			Replace			Inspect
Spark Plugs Wires			Check			Check			Check
PCV Valve			Replace			Replace			Replace
PCV System Hoses & Tubes			Clean			Clean			Clean
Fuel System Filter						Replace			Replace
Fuel Lines & Connections						Inspect			Inspect

1974 MAINTENANCE SCHEDULE (continued)

MAINTENANCE INTERVALS
MILEAGE IN THOUSANDS, OR TIME IN MONTHS, WHICHEVER OCCURS FIRST

	4	8	12	16	20	24
Coolant Condition and Protection		Check		Check		Check
Cooling System Hoses and Clamps				Check		Replace
All Drive Belts	Check	Inspect		Inspect		Inspect
Distributor Cap and Rotor			Inspect			Inspect
Evaporative Emission Canister				Inspect		
Rear Axle Fluid Level	Check	Check	Check	Check	Check	Check
Trans. Fluid Level	Check	Check	Check	Check	Check	Check
Brake Fluid Level	Check	Check	Check	Check	Check	Check
Power Steering Fluid Level	Check	Check	Check	Check	Check	Check
Clutch Pedal Free Play	Adjust	Adjust	Adjust	Adjust	Adjust	Adjust
Brake Linings				Inspect		
Front Wheel Bearings				Clean & Repack		
Front Suspension and Ball Joints						Lubricate

10

1974 MAINTENANCE SCHEDULE

MAINTENANCE INTERVALS
MILEAGE IN THOUSANDS, OR TIME IN MONTHS, WHICHEVER OCCURS FIRST

	6	12	18	24	30	36
Engine Oil	Change	Change	Change	Change	Change	Change
Engine Oil Filter	Replace		Replace			Replace
Crankcase Breather Cap (If So Equipped)		Clean		Clean		Clean
Crankcase Emission Filter in Air Cleaner		Check		Replace		Check
Carburetor Air Cleaner Element		Check		Replace		Check
Exhaust Control Valve (If So Equipped) at Each Oil Change	Lube & Free-Up	Lube & Free-Up	Lube & Free-Up	Lube & Free-Up	Lube & Free-Up	Lube & Free-Up
Spark Plugs						
Breakerless Distributor		Replace All		Replace All		Replace All
Conventional Distributor		Replace All		Replace All		Replace All
Initial Ignition Timing	Adjust	Adjust	Adjust	Adjust		Adjust
Distributor Points—Conventional Distributor Only	Inspect	Inspeck	Inspect	Replace	Inspect	
Spark Plug Wires			Inspect	Inspect	Inspect	Inspect
PCV Valve				Replace		Replace
PCV System, Hoses and Tubes		Check		Clean		Check
Fuel System Filter						Replace

1975 MAINTENANCE SCHEDULE

("A" and "B" schedules have been combined. Use the letter that matches the one found on your engine decal or glove box label).

MAINTENANCE OPERATION	SERVICE INTERVAL—Time in months or mileage in thousands, whichever occurs first.						
	5	10	15	20	25	30	35
Change Engine Oil	AB	AB	AB	AB	AB	AB	AB
Replace Engine Oil Filter	AB		AB		AB		AB
Torque Intake Manifold Bolts (302/351W)			B	A			
Lubricate and Check Exhaust COntrol Valve			B	A		B	
Check Coolant Condition and Proection			B	A			
Replace Coolant							AB
Check Cooling System Hoses and Clamps							AB
Check Drive Belt Tension			B	A			
Inspect Drive Belt Condition						B	
Replace PCV Valve				A		B	
Check PCV System, Hoses and Tubes			B	A			
Clean PCV System, Hoses and Tubes				A		B	
Replace Crankcase Filter in Air Cleaner				A		B	
Inspect Evaporative Emission Canister				A		B	
Inspect Fuel Vapor System (Fuel tank filler cap, hoses and vapor lines)				A		B	
Replace Spark Plugs			B	A		B	
Spark Plug Wires			B	A		B	
Check Initial Ignition TIming			B	A		B	
Distributor Cap and Rotor			B	A		B	
Check Carburetor Air Cleaner Element			B				
Replace Carburetor Air Cleaner Element				A		B	
Replace Fuel System Filter			B	A			
Check Rear Axle Fluid Level	AB		AB		AB		AB
Check Trans. Fluid Level	AB		AB		AB		AB
Check Brake Master Cylinder Fluid Level	AB		AB		AB		AB
Lubricate Front Suspension						AB	
Check Brake Linings, Front Wheel Bearings					AB		

1976 MAINTENANCE SCHEDULE

(This chart applies to cars on schedules "A" & "B". Letter can be found on decal or glove box label).

MAINTENANCE OPERATION	SERVICE INTERVAL—Time in months or mileage in thousands, whichever occurs first.						
	5	10	15	20	25	30	35
Change Engine Oil	AB	AB	AB	AB	AB	AB	AB
Replace Engine Oil Filter	AB		AB		AB		AB
Lubricate and Check Exhaust Control Valve			B	A		B	
Check Coolant Condition and Protection			B	A			
Replace Coolant							AB
Check Cooling System Hoses and Clamps							AB
Check Drive Belt Tension			B	A			
Inspect Drive Belt Condition						B	
Replace PCV Valve				A		B	
Check PCV System Hoses and Tubes			B	A			
Clean PCV System Hoses and Tubes				A		B	
Replace Crankcase Filter in Air Cleaner				A		B	
Inspect Evaporative Emission Canister				A		B	
Inspect Fuel Vapor System (Fuel tank filler, cap, hoses and vapor lines)				A		B	
Replace Spark Plugs			B	A		B	
Visually Inspect Spark Plug Wires			B	A		B	
Check Initial Ignition Timing	AB						
Visually Inspect Distributor Cap and Rotor			B	A		B	
Check Carburetor Air Cleaner Element			B				
Replace Carburetor Air Cleaner Element				A		B	
Replace Fuel System Filter		AB					
Check Brake Master Cylinder Fluid Level						AB	
Check Clutch Pedal Free Play Adjust, if required		AB		AB		AB	
Inspect Brake Lining, Lines, Hoses and front wheel bearing lube						AB	
Lubricate Front Suspension and Steering Linkage						AB	

1976 MAINTENANCE SCHEDULE

(This chart applies to cars on schedule "C." Letter can be found on decal or glove box label).

MAINTENANCE OPERATION	SERVICE INTERVAL—Time in months or mileage in thousands, whichever occurs first.					
	6	12	18	24	30	36
Change engine oil	C	C	C	C	C	C
Replace engine oil filter	C		C		C	
Replace crankcase emission filter in air cleaner				C		
Check carburetor air cleaner element			C			C
Replace carburetor air cleaner element				C		
Inspect fuel vapor emissions control system (fuel tank filler cap, hoses and vapor lines				C		
Replace all spark plugs			C			C
Adjust initial ignition timing			C			C
Inspect spark plug wires			C			C
Replace PCV Valve				C		
Check operation of PCV system, hoses and tubes			C			C
Clean PCV system, hoses and tubes				C		
Replace fuel system filter	C					
Check coolant condition and protection			C	C		
Replace coolant						C
Check cooling system hoses and clamps				C		
Check all drive belts	C					
Inspect all drive belts	C	C		C		C
Inspect distributor cap and rotor			C			C
Inspect evaporative emission canister				C		
Check brake master cylinder fluid level—add fluid if required					C	
Lubricate front suspension and ball joints						C
Inspect brake linings, lines, hoses and front wheel bearing lube					C	
Check clutch pedal free play—adjust if required	C	C	C	C	C	C

1977 MAINTENANCE SCHEDULE

(This chart applies to cars on schedule "A" or "B". Letter is found on decal)

MAINTENANCE SCHEDULES A and B (Schedules A and B have been Combined into one chart. Follow the Schedule which corresponds to your car's code letter.)	SERVICE INTERVAL—TIME IN MONTHS OR MILES IN THOUSANDS, WHICHEVER OCCURS FIRST, UNLESS OTHERWISE SPECIFIED.					
MAINTENANCE OPERATION						
MONTHS/MILES	**7.5**	**15**	**22.5**	**30**	**37.5**	**45**
Change Engine Oil	AB	AB	AB	AB	AB	AB
Replace Engine Oil Filter	AB		AB		AB	
Replace Spark Plugs			A	B		A
Check Coolant Condition & Protection			ANNUALLY			
Replace Coolant						AB
Checking Cooling Sys., Hoses, & Clamps						AB
Check Drive Belt Tension	B		A	B		A
Replace PCV Valve if specified on engine decal. All others not required.			A	B		
Replace Carburetor Air Cleaner Element			AB			
Replace Crankcase Filter In Air Cleaner			AB			
Check Ingition Initial TIming (adjust as required)	AB					
Inspect brake lining, lines, hoses, and front wheel bearing lube			AB			
Check brake master cylinder fluid level			AB			

1977 MAINTENANCE SCHEDULE

(This chart applies to cars on schedule "C". Letter is found on decal).

MAINTENANCE SCHEDULE C	SERVICE INTERVAL—TIME IN MONTHS OR MILES IN THOUSANDS, WHICHEVER OCCURS FIRST, UNLESS OTHERWISE SPECIFIED.							
MAINTENANCE OPERATION								
MILES	**6**	**12**	**18**	**24**	**30**	**36**	**42**	**48**
Change Engine Oil	C	C	C	C	C	C	C	C
Replace Engine Oil Filter	C		C		C		C	
Replace All Spark Plugs (with Use of Low Lead or Unleaded Fuel)				C			C	
Replace All Spark Plugs (with use of Leaded Fuel)		C		C		C		C
Lube & Free-Up Exhaust Control Valve (if so equipped) at Each Oil Change	C	C	C	C	C	C	C	C

1977 MAINTENANCE SCHEDULE (continued)
(This chart applies to cars on schedule "C". Letter is found on decal).

MAINTENANCE SCHEDULE C MAINTENANCE OPERATION	SERVICE INTERVAL—TIME IN MONTHS OR MILES IN THOUSANDS, WHICHEVER OCCURS FIRST, UNLESS OTHERWISE SPECIFIED.							
MILES	6	12	18	24	30	36	42	48
Replace Crankcase Emission Filter in Air Cleaner				C				C
Check Carburetor Air Cleaner Element		C				C		
Replace Carburetor Air Cleaner Element				C				C
Inspect Fuel Vapor Emission Control System (Hoses, Vapor Lines, and Fuel Tank Filler Cap)				C				C
Adjust Initial Ignition Timing			C			C		
Inspect Spark Plug Wires (with Use of Low Lead or Unleaded Fuel)			C			C		
Inspect Spark Plug Wires (with Use of Leaded Fuel)		C		C		C		C
Replace PCV Valve				C				C
Clean PCV System, Hoses and Tubes				C				C
Check PCV System, Hoses and Tubes		C				C		
Replace Fuel System Filter	C							
Check Coolant Condition and Protection		C		C		C		C
Replace Cooling System Fluid						C		
Check Cooling System Hoses and Clamps				C				C
Inspect All Drive Belts (Check Tension at 6,000 Miles)	C	C		C		C		C
Inspect Distributor Cap and Rotor			C			C		
Inspect Evaporative Emission Canister (All)				C				C
Check Brake Master Cylinder					C			
Inspect Brake Lines and Linings and Front Wheel Bearings					C			
Lubricate Front Suspension and Steering Linkage						C		

and screw the new filter into place on the engine. Follow the instructions on the box of the new filter and *do not overtighten it. Use only your hands, no tools, to tighten the filter.* Dispose of the old oil in the large empty plastic bleach bottles generally found around every house. Do not pour the old oil down a water drain or sewer as it can pollute the water supply. Dispose of it in the trashcan. The oil is not flammable. Finally, refill the engine with the new oil making sure you do not forget the extra amount to be added for the filter. Consult the chart for the proper quantity but also, after filling the engine, use the dipstick to make sure it is filled to the proper level.

COOLING SYSTEM & CAPACITY DATA

Year	Model or Engine	Cooling Capacity, Qts. ③			Thermo. Opening Temp. ①	Fuel Tank Gals.	Engine Oil Refill Qts. ②
		No Heater	With Heater	With A/C			
1970	6-240	13½	14½	14½	195	24⑤	4
	8-302	13½	14½	14½	195	24⑤	4
	8-351	15½	16½	16½	195	24⑤	4
	8-390	19	20	20	195	24⑤	4
	8-429	17½	18½	18½	195	24⑤	4
1971	6-240	13	14	14	195	23⑤	4
	8-302	14	15	15	195	23⑤	4
	8-351	15¼	16¼	16¼	195	23⑤	
	8-390	19	20	20	195	23⑤	4
	8-400	16½	17½	18¼	195	23⑤	4
	8-429	18	19	19	195	23⑤	4
1972	6-240	13¼	14¼	14¼	195	22⑤	4
	8-302	14¼	15¼	15¼	195	22④	4
	8-351	15½	16½	16½	195	22④	4
	8-400	16¾	17¾	18¼	195	22④	4
	8-429	17¾	18¾	20	195	22④	4
1973	8-351C	14½	15½	16¼	195	22④	4
	8-351W	15½	16½	17	195	22④	4
	8-400	17	18	18	195	22④	4
	8-429	18½	19½	19½	195	22④	4
1974	8-351C	15.3	16½	17.2	191	22④	4
	8-351W	15.3	16½	16½	191	22④	4
	8-400	17	18	18½	191	22④	4
	8-460	18.4	19½	19½	191	22④	4
1975	8-351	—	17.1	17.6	191	24.2④	4
	8-400	—	17.1	17.6	191	24.2④	4
	8-460	—	18.5	18.5⑥	191	24.2④	4⑦
1976	8-351	16.3	17.1	17.6	191	24.2④	4
	8-400	16.3	17.1	17.6	191	24.2④	4
	8-460	—	18.5	18.5⑥	191	24.2④	4⑦

COOLING SYSTEM & CAPACITY DATA *(continued)*

Year	Model or Engine	Cooling Capacity, Qts. ③			Thermo. Opening Temp. ①	Fuel Tank Gals.	Engine Oil Refill Qts. ②
		No Heater	With Heater	With A/C			
1977	8-351	16.3	17.1	17.2	191	24.2④	4
	8-400	16.3	17.1	17.5	191	24.2④	4
	8-460	18.4	19.2	19.2	191	24.2④	4⑦

①—With permanent type anti-freeze.
②—Add one quart with filter change.
③—Radiator cap relief pressure: 1977 V8-460, 14-18 lbs. All others 12-15 lbs.
④—Station wagons 21 gals. Add 8 gals. with auxiliary tank.
⑤—Station wagons 22 gals.
⑥—Medium duty 19 qts. Heavy duty & Police 20 qts.
⑦—Police models 6½ qts.

COOLING SYSTEM SERVICE

One of the simplest services you can perform on you car would be to drain the cooling system of the old coolant and refill it with fresh all year coolant. More and more the name "anti-freeze" is disappearing from these containers and being replaced by the name "Summer/Winter coolant". Rightly so too, because these coolants do more than just prevent freezing in the winter. They also prevent boiling-over in the hot summer. Cars with air conditioners, especially, need this all year coolant or they will be likely candidates for overheating during the hot summer months. If the coolant in your car's radiator is dirty, rusty or contains particles of rubber or other contaminants, drain and flush it now and save the headache that could come while driving on the freeway.

It is good practice to thoroughly check every component in the cooling system at this time. Any hoses or belts that show signs of wear or cracks should be replaced now so you can be assured the system is in good order. Also, if you have been having trouble getting heat from the heater in cold weather it is advisable at this time to replace the thermostat with one of the proper opening temperature as listed in the chart.

Proceed as follows on a cold engine:

1. Open the radiator petcock at the bottom of the radiator, Fig.2, and allow the coolant to drain into a suitable pan. Remove the radiator cap to speed this process.
2. When completely drained, close the petcock and refill the radiator with plain water and a cooling system flush which can be purchased locally at any auto store.

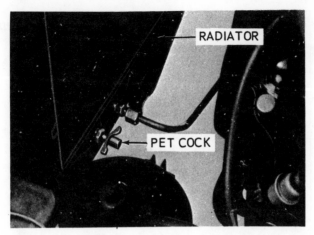

Fig. 2   Radiator petcock (draincock) location

3. Replace the cap and start the engine and allow it to run until warmed up. About 15 minutes should be enough.
4. Shut the engine off and allow the engine to cool thoroughly before attempting to remove the radiator cap.
5. When sufficiently cooled down again open the petcock and remove the radiator cap, allowing the system to drain. Removing the lower radiator hose at the radiator will help in draining the engine block.
6. When completely drained, close the radiator petcock, replace hose if removed, and refill the system with fresh coolant in at least a 50/50 solution of water mixed with the new coolant.
7. Start the engine and allow it to warm up and circulate the coolant to eliminate any air pockets in the system.
8. Fill the system again as needed

and wash off the radiator cap and it's seat in the radiator filler neck. Replace the cap and check the system for leaks.

THERMOSTAT REPLACEMENT

A thermostat which is stuck closed will quickly cause the engine to overheat, whereas one that is stuck open will be a cause of poor heater operation.

The thermostat is located in the elbow found at the engine side of the upper radiator hose. It should be replaced with one of the same opening temperature as listed in the chart. Here is how to replace it.

1. Drain the radiator so the coolant is below the level of the water outlet elbow.
2. Unfasten the elbow from the engine and pull it away enough to

19

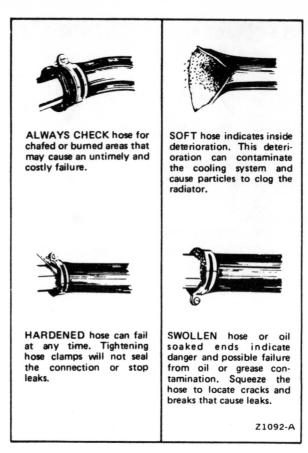

Fig. 3   Hose condition chart

ALWAYS CHECK hose for chafed or burned areas that may cause an untimely and costly failure.

SOFT hose indicates inside deterioration. This deterioration can contaminate the cooling system and cause particles to clog the radiator.

HARDENED hose can fail at any time. Tightening hose clamps will not seal the connection or stop leaks.

SWOLLEN hose or oil soaked ends indicate danger and possible failure from oil or grease contamination. Squeeze the hose to locate cracks and breaks that cause leaks.

Z1092-A

allow removal of the thermostat.

3. Before replacing the thermostat, make sure all of the old gasket is thoroughly cleaned from the elbow and the engine or a leak will result.

HOSE REPLACEMENT

Periodically, but at least at the beginning of Spring and Fall, make it a practice to inspect all hoses for crack-ing, rotting, extreme softness when squeezed, or questionable. It is a lot less trouble to inspect and replace hoses at your convenience than it is to find yourself away from home with a broken hose, no coolant, and an overheated engine. And, if one hose is found to be in poor condition it would be safe to assume that the rest of the hoses are pretty much in the same condition.

To replace hoses, proceed as follows:

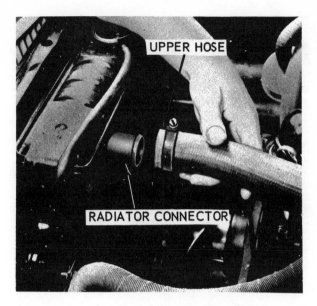

Fig. 4   Removing radiator hose

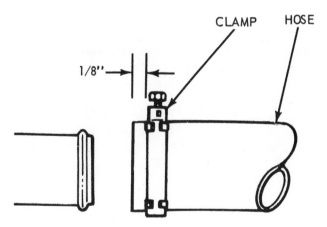

Fig. 5   Positioning clamp on hose

1. Drain the radiator into a suitable pan, by opening the petcock found at the bottom of the radiator. Remove the radiator cap to speed this process. When it is completely drained, close the petcock so you won't forget it later.

2. Loosen the clamps at each end of the hoses to be removed. This can be done quite easily with a

21

BEAD
UNDER HOSE

Fig. 6   Installing radiator hose

screwdriver but do not place your free hand beneath the clamp in case the screwdriver slips. If the clamps are old and of the wire type it would be well to replace the clamps.

3. Twist the hose back and forth to loosen the hose from the connector. Slide the hose off the connections when free, Fig. 4. If the hose is dried and cracked and remnants of it remain on the connectors, clean the connection thoroughly with a scraper or putty knife. Do not pry under the hose as the connector is soft and may be damaged.

4. Position the new clamps on the new hose at least ⅛″ from each end of the hose and slip the hose

on the connector, Fig. 5.

5. When tightening the clamps, be sure the clamp is positioned beyond the bead and in the center of the clamping surface of the connector, Fig. 6.

6. Add the fresh coolant in the proper amount as listed in the chart found on the container, to maintain protection.

DRIVE BELT REPLACEMENT

It is important to keep drive belts at the proper tension, not only to minimize noise and prolong service life of the belt, but also to protect the parts being driven by the belt. A loose

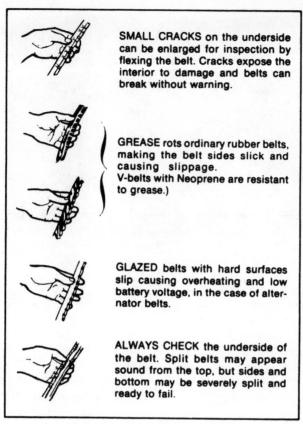

Fig. 7   Belt inspection chart

belt may cause improper alternator, fan and water pump operation whereas too tight a belt places a strain on the water pump and alternator bearings.

All belts should be inspected at regular 12 month intervals. Carefully examine the belts by turning a portion of the belt over so you can see the underside, Fig. 7. Belts that are frayed, cut, glazed or show uneven wear, should be replaced. It is also reasonable to assume, that if one belt requires replacement, the others may as well.

Replace belts as follows:

1. Loosen the pivot bolt on the unit such as the alternator, power steering pump or air conditioning compressor.
2. After loosening the bolts, force the unit toward the slack position. This will make it possible for the belt to be worked off the pulleys and over the fan.
3. When replacing the belts, install the rearward belt first and each belt in turn towards the outermost one.
4. When all belts are in position,

23

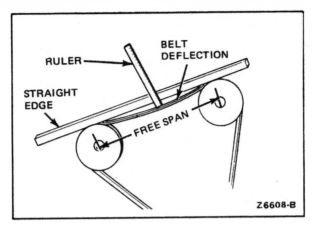

Fig. 8   Measuring belt deflection

begin to swing the units out to the tight position and tighten the pivot bolt. Using a ruler, depress the belt at the midpoint between the pulleys, the amount of deflection should be 4″. The belt is too loose if a squeal is heard when the accelerator is depressed rapidly.

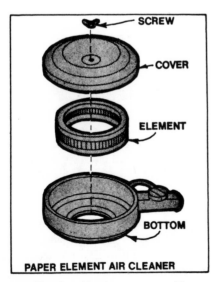

Fig. 9   Air cleaner assembly

AIR CLEANER ELEMENT REPLACEMENT

Clogged air filters contribute to poor engine performance and low gasoline mileage.

Check and replace the air cleaner element at the intervals recommended in the maintenance charts in the front of this book. The top of the air cleaner is secured by a wing nut, Fig. 9. Remove the wing nut and lift off the lid of the air cleaner. Then lift out the element and check it by looking through the element toward the light as shown in Fig. 10. If you can not see the light, the filter is dirty and should be replaced with one of of the same type.

FUEL FILTER REPLACEMENT

If your car hesitates or seems to miss at high speeds, check the fuel filter as it may be clogged. Fig. 11

shows two types of filters. The top one in the illustration is connected to the fuel line before the carburetor with two lengths of rubber hose and secured by wire clamps. The lower pictured filter is screwed into the carburetor and secured by a rubber hose and wire clamp on the other end. Replacement filters may have an arrow marked on the case to show the direction of fuel flow. This arrow should always point toward the carburetor.

Fig. 10   Checking condition of air cleaner element

TIRE CARE

Get in the habit of making tire inspection a part of your routine car check. Inspect tires for wear which may be caused by incorrect wheel alignment, improper tire pressure or an out of balance condition.

Tire pressure should be checked

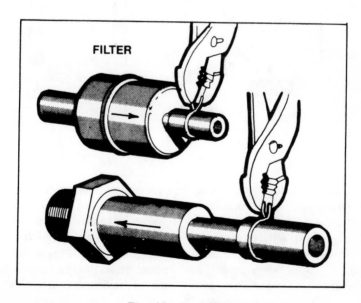

FILTER

Fig. 11   Fuel filter

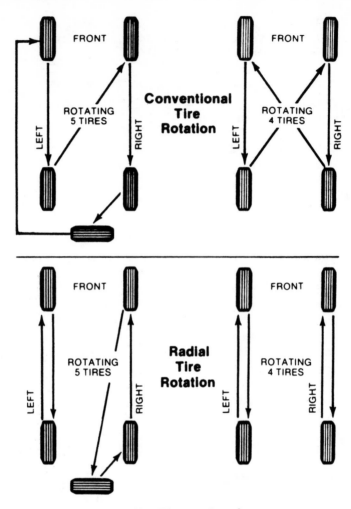

FRONT

ROTATING
5 TIRES

**Conventional
Tire
Rotation**

FRONT

ROTATING
4 TIRES

LEFT   RIGHT

FRONT

ROTATING
5 TIRES

**Radial
Tire
Rotation**

FRONT

ROTATING
4 TIRES

LEFT   RIGHT

Fig. 12   Tire rotation plans

while the tires are cold, before driving the car any distance. An out of balance tire and wheel assembly or improper wheel alignment will have to be checked by a skilled mechanic using equipment made for this purpose.

Tire rotation is as important to good tire life as any of the items mentioned

previously. Look at the various rotation plans shown in Fig. 12, and follow the plan that applies to your type of tire. Obviously your local garage can rotate tires quickly using a lift and power tools. But since the name of the game is saving money, let us show you a little tip that can save you money

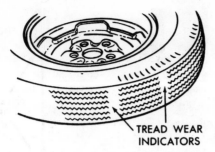

TREAD WEAR
INDICATORS

Fig. 13   Tread wear bars showing

twice a year. Think of how may times you may have had your local garage install and remove your snow tires. A small investment in a set of extra wheels, which can be bought at local salvage yards very cheaply, will enable you to install and remove your own snow tires quite easily. Simply have your snow tires mounted on the extra wheels. Then when it is time for their use, no special equipment will be needed.

Remember too, that studded snow tires must always be placed in the same position on the car so when you remove them be sure they are marked either right or left.

Most importantly, replace any tire that is worn to the point that the tread wear bars are showing, Fig. 13. Statistics show that 90% of all flats and blowouts occur in the last 10% of tire life so by replacing tires that are excessively worn you can avoid the upset of having a tire problem on the road when you least expect it. Having to purchase a tire under these conditions can be costly whereas replacing it beforehand will allow you to shop and take advantage of the many tire sales offered locally by tire chains or department stores.

Tune Up

Why do we need a tune up? The whole idea of keeping the engine in proper tune is more important today than it ever was in the past. The scarcity of fuels makes it necessary for us to change our old habits.

You benefit directly by keeping your car in good running condition. It will operate more efficiently, which simply means more miles per gallon or less money out of your pocket each time you pull up to the gas pump. And the air we all breathe will be cleaner because of this better running engine.

Don't be afraid that you might not have the ability to do this kind of work. We are going to be helping you. These straightforward routines are easily understood and by their nature will save you money.

Spark plugs and all ignition parts can be purchases at local department stores at greatly reduced prices. The Ford came equipped with Autolite spark plugs of the designation shown in the chart. All suppliers may not carry all brands of spark plugs but your supplier will have a cross reference chart which will enable him to supply you with another kind of spark plug having the same qualities.

If the engine is using too much oil, a compression test should be taken. If the engine compression is normal, then the lowest reading cylinder will be at least 75% of the highest reading cylinder with no cylinder reading lower than 100 lbs. If the engine does not meet these requirements a tune-up will do little to help and you must decide whether you should consult a professional mechanic about having the engine overhauled. It might be more economical to swap the engine, if you can locate an engine at a salvage yard from a wrecked car.

Here's how to test compression: Label each of the spark plug wires so you can easily identify which plug they were removed from Then remove the air cleaner assembly. Brush away any dirt around the bottom of the spark plugs before removing them. Block the choke valve and the trottle valve in the wide open position. Remove the thick wire from the center of the ignition coil. This wire also leads to the center of the distributor cap. Obtain a compression gauge and install it into one of the spark plug holes. Using the ignition key, crank the engine about four revolutions and record the reading from the gauge. Continue this process until all of the cylinders have been checked. Compare the readings, If readings are low, squirt about a tablespoonful of engine oil into the cylinders at the holes where the spark plugs belong. Check the compression again. If the readings are now much higher, worn piston rings are indicated and an engine overhaul may be in order. If the readings do not improve, burned valves or valves not seating properly may be the likely cause and a valve job may be needed. If low reading are obtained from two adjacent cylinders, the cause may be a leaky head gasket which would permit coolant to get into the engine oil or engine oil into the coolant. This could lead to serious internal engine damage.

SPARK PLUG SERVICE

Spark plugs should normally be replaced every 12,000 miles but they may last considerably longer on cars having catalytic converters and using non-leaded fuels. Consult the maintenance services chart in the front of this book.

Before removing any spark plugs, label each of the wires leading to the plugs in a fashion that will enable you to get the wires back on the correct plugs. You might tag them with numbers such as 1, 2, 4, 5, 6 from front to rear or in the case of a V8 engine you might tag them 1-R meaning first cylinder on the right or passenger's side of the car. Use a system you are comfortable with to get the wires back in their correct positions. You might also choose to remove only one spark plug at time thereby having only one wire disconnected at a time and minimizing the chance of error.

Proceed as follows:

1. After tagging the wires, remove them carefully from the spark plugs. Do not pull on the wires. Grasp the rubber boot down at the spark plug and twist it to free it from the plug. Then pry carefully with your fingertip to lift the boot from the spark plug.

2. Brush away any dirt around the spark plugs and using a socket, extension and ratchet, remove all of the spark plugs.

3. Check the condition of the old spark plugs by comparing them to the chart, Fig. 14.

4. If the old spark plugs are to be reused, file the electrodes, Fig. 15, using an ignition point file. Be sure all deposits are cleaned from inside the shell and inspect them to make sure the porcelain is clean and not cracked. Replace any spark plug that has been dropped

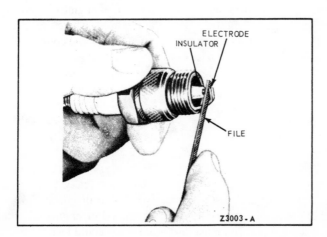

Fig. 15   Filing spark plug electrodes

GAP BRIDGED	OIL FOULED	CARBON FOULED

IDENTIFIED BY DEPOSIT BUILD-UP CLOSING GAP BETWEEN ELECTRODES CAUSED BY OIL OR CARBON FOULING. IF DEPOSITS ARE NOT EXCESSIVE, THE PLUG CAN BE CLEANED	IDENTIFIED BY WET BLACK DEPOSITS ON THE INSULATOR SHELL BORE ELECTRODES CAUSED BY EXCESSIVE OIL ENTERING COMBUSTION CHAMBER THROUGH WORN RINGS AND PISTONS, EXCESSIVE CLEARANCE BETWEEN VALVE GUIDES AND STEMS, OR WORN OR LOOSE BEARINGS. CAN BE CLEANED IF ENGINE IS NOT REPAIRED, USE A HOTTER PLUG	IDENTIFIED BY BLACK, DRY FLUFFY CARBON DEPOSITS ON INSULATOR TIPS, EXPOSED SHELL SURFACES AND ELECTRODES. CAUSED BY TOO COLD A PLUG, WEAK IGNITION, DIRTY AIR CLEANER, DEFECTIVE FUEL PUMP, TOO RICH A FUEL MIXTURE, IMPROPERLY OPERATING HEAT RISER OR EXCESSIVE IDLING. CAN BE CLEANED.
WORN	NORMAL	LEAD FOULED

IDENTIFIED BY SEVERELY ERODED OR WORN ELECTRODES CAUSED BY NORMAL WEAR SHOULD BE REPLACED	IDENTIFIED BY LIGHT TAN OR GRAY DEPOSITS ON THE FIRING TIP CAN BE CLEANED	IDENTIFIED BY DARK GRAY, BLACK, YELLOW OR TAN DEPOSITS OR A FUSED GLAZED COATING ON THE INSULATOR TIP. CAUSED BY HIGHLY LEADED GASOLINE. CAN BE CLEANED.
PRE-IGNITION	OVERHEATING	FUSED SPOT DEPOSIT

IDENTIFIED BY MELTED ELECTRODES AND POSSIBLY BLISTERED INSULATOR. METALLIC DEPOSITS ON INSULATOR INDICATE ENGINE DAMAGE. CAUSED BY WRONG TYPE OF FUEL, INCORRECT IGNITION TIMING OR ADVANCE, TOO HOT A PLUG, BURNT VALVES OR ENGINE OVERHEATING. REPLACE THE PLUG.	IDENTIFIED BY A WHITE OR LIGHT GRAY INSULATOR WITH SMALL BLACK OR GRAY BROWN SPOTS AND WITH BLUISH-BURNT APPEARANCE OF ELECTRODES, CAUSED BY ENGINE OVERHEATING, WRONG TYPE OF FUEL, LOOSE SPARK PLUGS, TOO HOT A PLUG, LOW FUEL PUMP PRESSURE OR INCORRECT IGNITION TIMING. REPLACE THE PLUG.	IDENTIFIED BY MELTED OR SPOTTY DEPOSITS RESEMBLING BUBBLES OR BLISTERS. CAUSED BY SUDDEN ACCELERATION. CAN BE CLEANED

Fig. 14   Spark plug condition chart

or has a cracked porcelain. Check the gap (air space) between the two electrodes at the bottom of the threaded end, using a wire gauge, Fig. 16. Adjust the gap by bending the side electrode, Fig. 17, to the dimension shown in the chart.

5. If new spark plugs are being installed, it is a good practice to also check the gaps as they are not always correct.

6. Screw the spark plugs back into the holes. To properly thread the spark plugs, use your fingers first to screw them in position before you tighten them with the socket wrench. Replace the spark plug wires according to the tags previously placed on the wires.

7. Start the engine to make sure it is running properly. A shaking or rough running engine might mean that the wires are not pushed onto the spark plugs tightly enough.

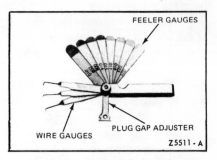

Fig. 16   Typical feeler gauge

SPARK PLUG WIRES

These wires should be inspected at regular intervals and preferably at tune-up time, to determine if they are oil soaked, cracked or burned. If they are in need of replacement, new wires can be purchased at most automotive counters in large department stores. Try to obtain wires that are exact replacements for your car. Such sets will

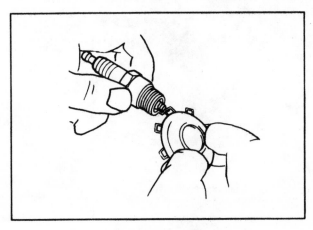

Fig. 17   Adjusting spark plug gap

have the wires cut to correct lengths and contain the terminals on both ends of the wires. Universal sets, which are more readily available, will only have the spark plug boot end attached to the wire. You will then have to cut the wire to proper length and attach the terminal and boot on the other end which goes into the distributor cap.

To replace wires on universal sets, proceed as follows:

1. Remove the longest wire first. This will usually be the wire leading to the spark plug furthest away from the distributor.
2. Match this wire to the longest wire of the new set and cut it to length, if necessary.
3. Slip the boot on the unfinished end and then affix the terminal.

4. Replace this new wire to the spark plug in the same routing as the old wire and push it firmly into the distributor cap. Then slip the boot tightly over the cap tower.
5. Continue replacing the rest of the wires in this fashion.

DISTRIBUTOR SERVICE

Beginning with mid 1974 production and all later models, a Breakerless Ignition System is used which greatly reduces the need for regular servicing on the distributor. However, these systems still use a conventional rotor and distributor cap so therefore these items

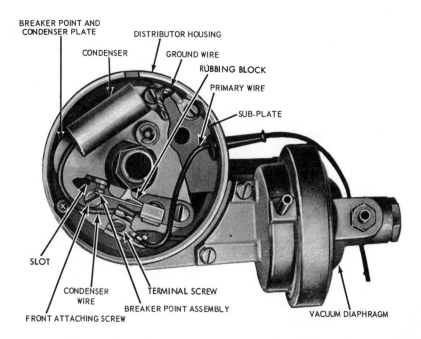

Fig. 18   Six cylinder distributor details

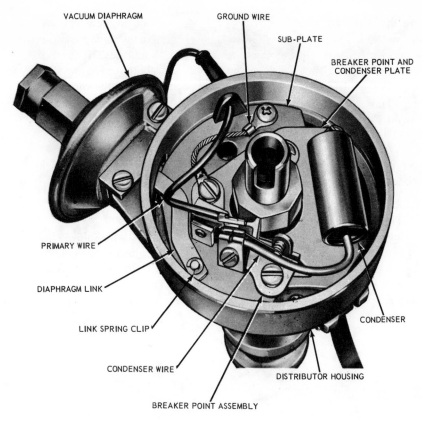

VACUUM DIAPHRAGM   GROUND WIRE

SUB-PLATE

BREAKER POINT AND
CONDENSER PLATE

PRIMARY WIRE

DIAPHRAGM LINK

LINK SPRING CLIP

CONDENSER WIRE

CONDENSER

DISTRIBUTOR HOUSING

BREAKER POINT ASSEMBLY

Fig. 19   V8 distributor details. (Single points)

must still be attended. Older models use the conventional breaker point ignition system and these require attention at least every 10,000 miles.

ELECTRONIC IGNITION

If your Ford is a mid 1974 or newer model, it does not contain ignition or breaker points and so you are spared this part of the routine servicing. If this system should fail it will require testing by a skilled auto mechanic using special equipment. Never remove any spark plug wires when the engine is

running as the higher voltages produced by this system may result in a severe shock. The distributor cap and rotor are replaced in the same manner as those for the conventional breaker point systems.

BREAKER POINT SYSTEMS

These systems can be expected to deliver good service if they are attended to at least every 10,000 miles. Breaker points and condensers should be replaced together to avoid the pos-

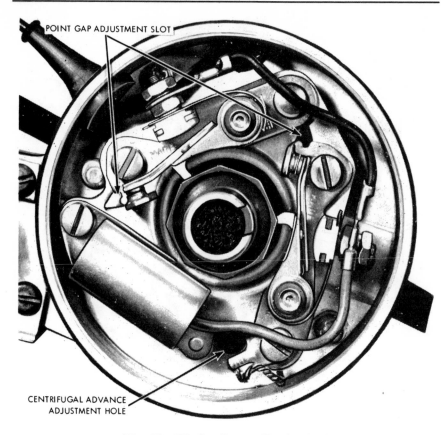

POINT GAP ADJUSTMENT SLOT

CENTRIFUGAL ADVANCE
ADJUSTMENT HOLE

Fig. 20   V8 distributor. (Dual points)

sibility that a poor condenser will quickly burn up a new set of points.

Here's how you can replace breaker points and condenser:

1. Disconnect the battery ground cable to prevent accidental shorts.
2. Unfasten the distributor cap from the distributor. The cap is secured by two bale clips which can be snapped off using a screwdriver.
3. Pull the rotor off the top of the distributor shaft. Notice that the underside of the rotor has an indexing tang which prevents it from being installed wrong.
4. Loosen the screw on the point set and disconnect the primary and condenser wires from the breaker point set, Figs. 18, 19 and 20.
5. Unfasten and remove the breaker points and condenser attaching screws and remove the points and condenser from the distributor. Notice location of ground wire. It goes under the attaching screw of the points furthest from the contacts on V8 engines and under the condenser attaching screw on six cylinder engines.
6. Wipe off the distributor cam and

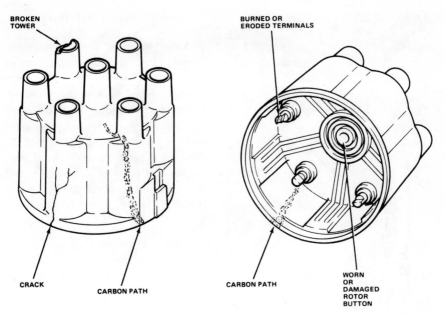

BROKEN
TOWER

BURNED OR
ERODED TERMINALS

CRACK   CARBON PATH   CARBON PATH   WORN
OR
DAMAGED
ROTOR
BUTTON

Fig. 21   Distributor cap inspection

breaker plate and apply a light coating of cam lube to the distributor cam.

7. Install the new point set and condenser being sure to return the ground wire under the proper attaching screw. Snug up the screws.

8. Connect the primary and condenser leads to the point set.

9. Put a rag over the fan blade, to protect your hands, and turn the fan clockwise to position the point set rubbing block squarely on the high point of one of the distributor cam lobes. This opens the point set gap to its widest openig.

10. Using a flat bladed feeler gauge of the correct size as listed in the chart, place it squarely between the points. If adjustment if re-quired, slightly loosen the point set attaching screws and insert the screwdriver tip in the notch beside the points and twist to open or close points for adjustment. When properly adjusted, the correct feeler gauge should pass the points with a slight touching between points and feeler. Tighten screws when correct spacing is obtained.

11. Install the rotor and distributor cap and reconnect the battery ground cable.

DISTRIBUTOR CAP & ROTOR REPLACEMENT

At tune-up time it is a good idea to check the condition of the distributor

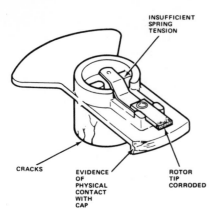

INSUFFICIENT
SPRING
TENSION

CRACKS

EVIDENCE
OF
PHYSICAL
CONTACT
WITH
CAP

ROTOR
TIP
CORRODED

Fig. 22   Rotor inspection

cap and rotor. Too often these items are merely taken for granted and assumed to be OK when they may be the cause for an engine miss due to a minute crack or carbon tracking, Fig. 21, or a worn rotor tip, Fig. 22. Carefully examine these parts and if the cap needs replacing get a new rotor at the same time. Replace the cap as follows:

1. Unfasten the distributor cap from the distributor and leave the wires plugged into it.
2. Hold the new cap next to the old cap in the same relative position.
3. Then carefully remove one wire from the old cap and install it into its same relative hole in the new cap. By following this procedure of replacing one wire at a time, there is little possibility for error in getting the wires into the wrong cap holes.
4. When completed, pull the old rotor off the distributor shaft and push the new rotor into place.
5. Install the new cap on the distributor in the same relative position as the old one occupied.

SETTING TIMING

After replacing distributor points and condenser, the ignition timing must be reset so your Ford can once again achieve its maximum performance level. Cars with Breakerless Ignition System (electronic ignition) do not require a timing check once the timing has been set correctly. If your car has lost some of its pep, it would be a good idea to check the timing as it may have been altered at a previous servicing.

Proceed as follows:

1. Hook up the timing light according to the instructions supplied with the light.
2. Remember that the number one cylinder is the front cylinder on six cylinder engines and it is the first cylinder on the right or passenger's side of V8 engines.
3. Wipe off the timing indicator and apply a dab of white paint to the notch on the pulley or vibration damper and also on the correct timing setting mark on the indicator tab.
4. Tag and remove any vacuum hoses from the vacuum diaphragm at the distributor. Plug the ends of these hoses with the pointed end of a pencil or a golf tee.
5. Start the engine and aim the light at the timing indicator. Some timing lights will make it necessary to perform this operation in a very dark place so the light flash can be observed.
6. Loosen the distributor hold-down bolt found at the very bottom of the distributor and rotate the distributor as necessary to align the

proper timing mark with the notch. It may be necessary to slow down the idle speed in order to make sure there is no distributor advance taking place.

7. When the timing is set, tighten the distributor hold-down bolts and then reset the idle speed, if previously altered.

8. Shut off the engine and remove the timing light and reconnect the vacuum hoses.

TUNE UP SPECIFICATIONS

The following specifications are published from the latest information available. This data should be used only in the absence of a decal affixed in the engine compartment.

★ When using a timing light, disconnect vacuum hose or tube at distributor and plug opening in hose or tube so idle speed will not be affected.

● When checking compression, lowest cylinder must be within 75% of the highest.

Year	Spark Plug		Distributor		Ignition Timing★ ①	Carb. Adjustments	
						Hot Idle Speed②	
	Type	Gap Inch	Point Gap Inch	Dwell Angle Deg.		Std. Trans.	Auto. Trans.②
1970							
6-240	BF-42	.035	③	③	6° ④	775/500	500
V8-302	BF-42	.035	.021	24–29	6° ⑤	775/500	575
V8-351	BF-42	.035	.021	24–29	6° ⑥	775/500	575
V8-390 Std. Tr.	BF-42	.035	.021	24–29	6° ⑤	775/500	—
V8-390 Auto. Tr.	BF-42	.035	.017	26–31	6° ⑤	—	600/500
V8-429 2 Bar. Carb.	BF-42	.035	.021	24–29	4° ⑤	—	600/500
V8-429 4 Bar. Carb.	BF-42	.035	⑬	⑬	4° ⑤	700	600
1971							
6-240	BRF-42	.034	.027	35–40	6° ④	800/500	500
V8-302 L/Air Cond.	BRF-42	.034	.021	24–29	6° ⑤	800/500	575
V8-302 w/Air Cond.	BRF-42	.034	.021	24–29	6° ⑤	800/500	600/500
V8-351W L/Air Cond.	BRF-42	.034	.021	24–29	6° ⑥	700/500	575
V8-351W w/Air Cond.	BRF-42	.034	.021	24–29	6° ⑥	700/500	600/500
V8-351C	ARF-42	.034	.021	24–29	6° ⑥	775/500	600/500
V8-390	BRF-42	.034	.021	24–29	6° ⑤	—	600/500
V8-400	ARF-42	.034	.021	24–29	⑦ ⑥	—	600/500
V8-429⑦ L/Air Cond.	BRF-42	.034	.021	24–29	6° ⑤	—	590
V8-429⑦ w/Air Cond.	BRF-42	.034	.021	24–29	6° ⑤	—	600/500
V8-429⑥	BRF-42	.034	.021	24–29	4° ⑤	700	600

TUNE UP SPECIFICATIONS *(continued)*

The following specifications are published from the latest information available. This data should be used only in the absence of a decal affixed in the engine compartment.

★ **When using a timing light, disconnect vacuum hose or tube at distributor and plug opening in hose or tube so idle speed will not be affected.**

● **When checking compression, lowest cylinder must be within 75% of the highest.**

Year	Spark Plug		Distributor		Ignition Timing★ ①	Carb. Adjustments Hot Idle Speed②	
	Type	Gap Inch	Point Gap Inch	Dwell Angle Deg.		Std. Trans.	Auto. Trans.②
1972							
6-240	BRF-42	.034	.027	35–39	6° ④	—	500
V8-302 w/Air Cond.	BRF-42	.034	.017	26–30	6° ⑤	800/500	600/500
V8-302 L/Air Cond.	BRF-42	.034	.017	26–30	6° ⑤	—	575
V8-351W w/Air Cond.	BRF-42	.034	.017	26–30	6° ⑥	—	600/500
V8-351W L/Air Cond.	BRF-42	.034	.017	26–30	6° ⑥	—	575
V8-351C	ARF-42	.034	.017	26–30	6° ⑥	—	700/500
V8-351C Calif.	ARF-42	.034	.017	26–30	6° ⑥	—	625/500
V8-400	ARF-42	.034	.017	26–30	⑧ ⑥	—	625/500
V8-429	BRF-42	.034	.017	26–30	10° ⑤	—	600/500
1973							
V8-351W	BRF-42	.034	.017	26–30	6° ⑥	—	600
V8-351W	ARF-42	.034	.017	26–30	10° ⑥	—	600
V8-400	ARF-42	.034	.017	26–31	6° ⑥	—	625
V8-429	ARF-42	.034	.017	26–30	10° ⑤	—	600
V8-460	ARF-42	.034	.017	26–30	10° ⑤	—	650
1974							
V8-351W	BRF-42	.044	.017	26–30	6° ⑥	—	600
V8-351W	BRF-42	.044	Electronic		6° ⑥	—	600
V8-351C	ARF-42	.044	.017	26–30	14° ⑥	—	650
V8-351C	ARF-42	.044	Electronic		14° ⑥	—	650
V8-400	ARF-42	.044	Electronic		12 ⑥	—	625
V8-460	ARF-52	.054	Electronic		⑨ ⑤	—	⑪
1975							
V8-351	ARF-42	.044	Electronic		14° ⑥	—	700D
V8-400	ARF-42	.044	Electronic		12° ⑥	—	625D
V8-460	ARF-52	.044	Electronic		14° ⑤	—	650D

TUNE UP SPECIFICATIONS *(continued)*

The following specifications are published from the latest information available. This data should be used only in the absence of a decal affixed in the engine compartment.

★ **When using a timing light, disconnect vacuum hose or tube at distributor and plug opening in hose or tube so idle speed will not be affected.**

● **When checking compression, lowest cylinder must be within 75% of the highest.**

Year	Spark Plug		Distributor		Ignition Timing★ ①	Carb. Adjustments Hot Idle Speed②	
	Type	Gap Inch	Point Gap Inch	Dwell Angle Deg.		Std. Trans.	Auto. Trans.②
1976							
V8-351	ARF-42	.044	Electronic		8° ⑥	—	650D
V8-400	ARF-42	.044	Electronic		10° ⑥	—	⑩
V8-460	ARF-52	.044	Electronic		10° ⑤	—	650D
1977							
V8-351	ARF-52	.050	Electronic		⑫	—	650D
V8-400 2 Bar. Carb.	ARF-52	.050	Electronic		⑫	—	⑩
V8-460	ARF-52	.050	Electronic		⑫	—	650D

①— Timing marks located on front cover.
②— Where two speeds are listed, the lower speed is with the throttle solenoid disconnected.
③— With dual diaphragm vacuum control, point gap is .027"; dwell is 35°–40°. With single diaphragm vacuum control, point gap is .025"; dwell is 37°–42°.
④— Firing order 1-5-3-6-2-4. Cylinders numbered front to rear.
⑤— Firing order 1-5-4-2-6-3-7-8. Cylinders numbered fron to rear right bank (passenger's side) 1-2-3-4. Left bank 5-6-7-8.
⑥— Firing order 1-3-7-2-6-5-4-8. Cylinders numbered front to rear right bank (passenger's side) 1-2-3-4. Left bank 5-6-7-8.
⑦— California models 6°, all others 10°.
⑧— California models 6°, all others 8°.
⑨— Police Interceptor 10°, all others 14°.
⑩— California models 625D, all others 650D.
⑪— Police Interceptor 700, all others 650.
⑫— Must refer to decal on car due to production changes.
⑬— With dual diaphragm vacuum control, point gap is .021", dwell is 24°-29°. With single diaphragm vacuum control, point gap is .017"; dwell is 26°-31°.

Fuel System

Dirt and water are a carburetor's enemies. Clogged air and fuel filters may allow dirt and water to pass thereby causing the carburetor to malfunction. This may appear as a hard starting problem or poor driveability at low or high speeds. In either event, the carburetor requires attention to cure the problem.

In this section, we will as a rule, provide instructions for adjusting the fuel level, float level and choke settings. Do not be afraid to bend the rods as indicated. They are not brittle and will bend quite easily using a needle nose pliers or similar tool.

CARBURETOR REMOVAL

This procedure is provided to help you in removing the carburetor so you can either disassemble it for cleaning or replace it with a new or rebuilt unit. If you are replacing it, be sure you obtain the replacement unit from a reputable auto parts store and be sure you fully understand the terms of any warranty that may be provided with the unit.

1. Disconnect the battery ground cable to prevent accidental shorts.
2. Remove the air cleaner assembly from the top of the carburetor.
3. Properly tag and disconnect all vacuum hoses, wires and linkage from the carburetor.
4. Disconnect the fuel line at the carburetor.
5. Remove the carburetor attaching bolts or nuts and lift the carburetor and gasket off the engine.
6. When replacing the carburetor, it is a good idea to also replace the fuel and air filters in the event they should be contaminated.
7. Install the replacement unit on the engine using a new gasket.
8. Replace and tighten the attaching bolts and reconnect the hoses and linkage and any wiring previously disconnected. Reconnect the fuel line.
9. Replace the air cleaner assembly and reconnect the battery ground cable.

CARBURETOR ADJUSTMENTS

The carburetor will rarely require attention if all systems are cared for and mainly that involves making sure the filters for the air cleaner and the fuel inlet are replaced at the required intervals. Consult the maintenance charts at the beginning of this book for those intervals

When it does become necessary to replace a carburetor or to disassemble it for cleaning, certain adjustments will have to be checked and perhaps altered as outlined in the following text on the various used on the Ford.

Do not be afraid to bend any rods to achieve the desired adjustment. These rods are not brittle and can be bent with very little force using a pair of long nose pliers.

HOW TO IDENTIFY YOUR CARBURETOR

*Number stamped on tag affixed to carburetor body

Year	Engine	Carb. Type	49 States*		California*	
			Man. Trans.	Auto. Trans.	Man. Trans.	Auto. Trans.
1970	6-240	YF	DOAF-A	DOAF-B	DOAF-A	DOAF-B
	V8-302	2100	DOAF-C	DOAF-D	DOAF-C	DOAF-D
	W/A.C.	2100	—	DOAF-U	—	DOAF-U
	V8-351	2100	DOAF-E	DOAF-F	DOAF-E	DOAF-F
	W/A.C.	2100	—	DOAF-V	—	DOAF-V
	V8-390	2100	DOAF-Y	DOAF-Z	DOAF-Y	DOAF-Z
	W/A.C.	2100	—	DOAF-AA	—	DOAF-AA
	V8-429	2100	—	DOAF-J	—	DOAF-J
	W/A.C.	2100	—	DOAF-T	—	DOAF-T
	V8-429	4300	DOAF-L, AB, AL	DOAF-AF, AM	DOAF-L, AB, AL	DOAF-AG, AM
1971	6-240	YF	DIAF-PA	DIAF-RA	DIAF-PA	DIAF-RA
	V8-302	2100	DIOF-ABA	DIAF-DA	DIOF-ABA	DIAF-DA
	W/A.C.	2100	—	DIZF-AA	—	DIZF-AA
	V8-351	2100	DIAF-FA	DIAF-JA	DIAF-FA	DIAF-JA
	W/A.C.	2100	—	DIAF-KA	—	DIAF-KA
	V8-390	2100	—	DIYF-DA	—	DIYF-DA
	V8-400	2100	—	DIMF-JA, KA	—	DIMF-JA, KA
	V8-429	2100	—	DIMF-FA	—	DIMF-FA
	V8-429	4300	—	DIAF-MA	—	DIAF-MA
1972	6-240	YF	—	D2AF-JA	—	D2AF-JA
	V8-302	2100	—	D2GF-AA	—	D2GF-AA

	Engine	No.		Carburetor		Carburetor
	V8-400	2100	—	D4ME-BA, CA	—	D4ME-BA, CA
	V8-460	4300	—	D4VE-AB	—	D4VE-AB
	V8-460	4300	—	D4AE-NA	—	D4AE-NA
	V8-460	4300	—	D4AE-AA	—	D4AE-AA
	V8-460	TQ	—	D4AE-BC	—	D4AE-BC
1975	V8-351	2150	—	D50E-BA	—	D50E-BA
	V8-351	2150	—	D50E-CA	—	D50E-CA
	V8-351	2150	—	D50E-GA	—	D50E-GA
	V8-400	2150	—	D5AE-AA	—	D5AE-AA
	V8-400	2150	—	D5AE-EA	—	D5AE-EA
	V8-400	2150	—	D5ME-BA	—	D5ME-BA
	V8-400	2150	—	D5ME-FA	—	D5ME-FA
	V8-400	2150	—	D5VE-AD	—	D5VE-AD
	V8-460	4350	—	D5VE-BA	—	D5VE-BA
	V8-460	4350	—	D5AE-CA	—	D5AE-CA
	V8-460	4350	—	D5AE-DA	—	D5AE-DA
1976	V8-460	4350	—	D5AE-DA	—	D5AE-DA
	V8-400	2150	—	D6WE-BA	—	D6ME-AA
	V8-460	4350	—	D6AE-HA	—	D6WE-AA
	V8-351	2150	—	D6WE-BA	—	D6AE-CA
	V8-460	4350	—	D6AE-DA	—	D6AE-CA
	V8-460	4350	—	—	—	D6AE-DA
	V8-460	4350	—	D6AE-CA	—	D6AE-CA
1977	V8-460	4350	—	D6AE-DA	—	D6AE-DA
	V8-460	2150	—	D6ME-AA	—	D6ME-AA
	V8-351W	2150	—	D70E-LA	—	D6WE-AA
	V8-351M	2150	—	D70E-RA	—	D7AE-AHA
	V8-400	2150	—	D70E-TA	—	D7AE-AKA
	V8-400 Altitude	2150	—	D7AE-ACA	—	—
	V8-460	4350	—	D7VE-SA	—	—

HOW TO IDENTIFY YOUR CARBURETOR (continued)

*Number stamped on tag affixed to carburetor body

Year	Engine	Carb. Type	49 States*		California*	
			Man. Trans.	Auto. Trans.	Man. Trans.	Auto. Trans.
1973	W/A.C.	2100	—	D2GF-BA	—	D2GF-BA
	V8-351W	2100	—	D2AF-FB	—	D2AF-FB
	W/A.C.	2100	—	D2AF-GB	—	D2AF-GB
	V8-351C	2100	—	D20F-UB	—	D20F-UB
	V8-351C	2100	—	D2WF-CA	—	—
	V8-400	2100	—	D2MF-FB	—	D2MF-FB
	V8-429	4300	—	D2AF-AA	—	—
	W/A.C.	4300	—	—	—	D2SF-BA
	V8-429	4300	—	D2AF-LA	—	D2AF-LA
	V8-351C	2100	—	D3AF-DC	—	D3AF-DC
	V8-351C	2100	—	D3AF-KA	—	D3AF-KA
	V8-351W	2100	—	D3AF-CE	—	D3AF-CE
	V8-400	2100	—	D3MF-AE	—	D3MF-AE
	V8-400	2100	—	D3MF-BA	—	D3MF-BA
	V8-429	4300	—	D3AF-HA	—	D3AF-HA
	V8-460	4300	—	D3AF-EB	—	D3AF-EB
	V8-460	4300	—	D3VF-DA	—	D3VF-DA
1974	V8-351W	2100	—	D4AE-DA, EA	—	D4AE-DA, EA
	V8-351C	2100	—	D40E-FA	—	D40E-FA
	V8-400	2100	—	D4AE-FA	—	D4AE-FA
	V8-400	2100	—	D4AE-GA, HB	—	D4AE-GA, HB

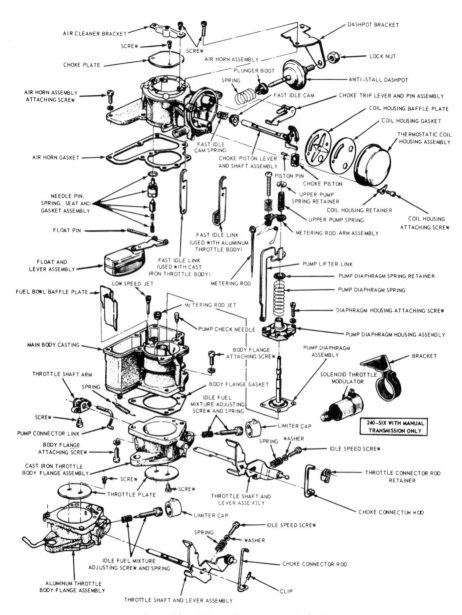

Fig. 23 YF carburetor exploded

YF CARBURETOR ADJUSTMENTS

Float Level

Referring to Fig. 24, turn the carburetor air horn upside down and check the clearance from the top of the float to the bottom of the air horn. The float lever arm should be resting on the needle pin. Bend the float arm as required to obtain the dimension listed in the chart.

Float Drop

Referring to Fig. 25, measure the clearance from the top of the float to the bottom of the air horn. Bend the tab at the end of the float arm to obtain the desired dimension as listed in the chart.

Dechoke Setting

Hold the throttle plate fully open and close the choke plate as far as possible without using force. Using a drill of the specified diameter as listed in the chart, measure the clearance betweenn the choke plate and the air horn, Fig. 26. Adjust the clearance by bending the arm of the choke trip lever portion of the throttle lever. Bending the arm downward will decrease the clearance while bending it upward will increase the clearance.

Pulldown Setting

Bend a .026″ diameter wire at a 90 degree angle about ⅛″ from one end. Insert the bent end of the wire between the choke piston slot and the right hand slot in the choke housing. Rotate the choke piston lever counterclockwise until the wire is snug in the piston slot. Exert a light pressure on the choke piston lever to hold the wire in place and then use a drill of the diameter as listed in the chart between the lower edge of

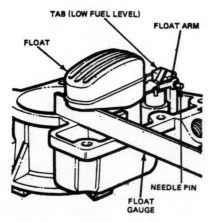

Fig. 24   YF float level adjustment

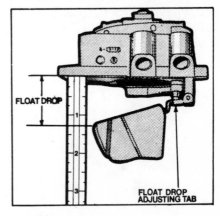

Fig. 25   YF float drop adjustment

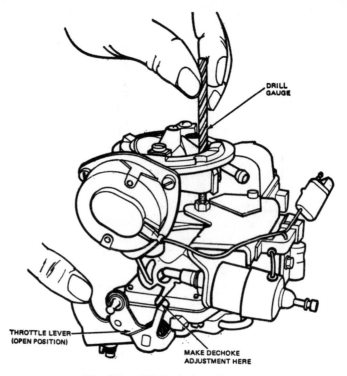

Fig. 26   YF dechoke adjustment

the choke plate and the carburetor bore, Fig. 27.

To adjust the clearance, bend the choke piston lever as required. When bending be careful not to distort the piston link.

Choke Setting

Loosen the choke cover retaining screws and turn the choke cover so that the line or index mark lines up with the specified mark on the housing. Consult the chart for the proper setting.

DRILL GAUGE

CHOKE PISTON
LEVER

.026"
WIRE
GAUGE

Fig. 27   YF pulldown setting

YF CARBURETOR ADJUSTMENT

*Number stamped on tag affixed to carburetor.

Year	Carb. No.*	Float Level	Float Drop	Dechoke Setting	Pulldown Setting	Choke Setting
1970	D0AF-A	3/8	1¼	.250	.225	Index
	D0AF-B	3/8	1¼	.250	.225	1 Lean
1971	D1AF-PA	3/8	1¼	.250	.200	Index
	D1AF-RA	3/8	1¼	.250	.230	Index
1972	D2AF-JA	3/8	1¼	.250	.230	1 Lean

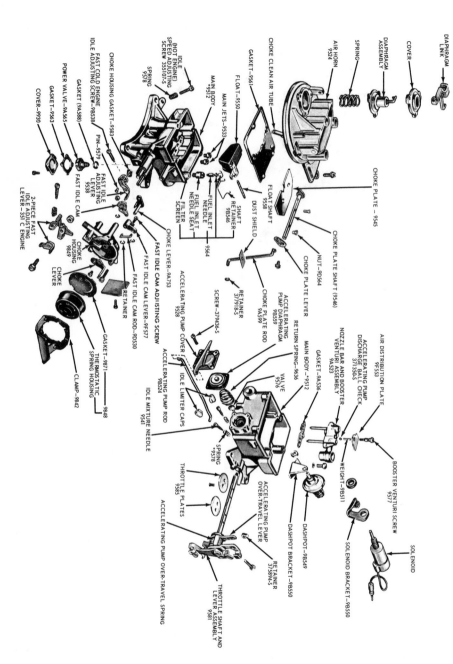

Fig. 28   2100 carburetor exploded

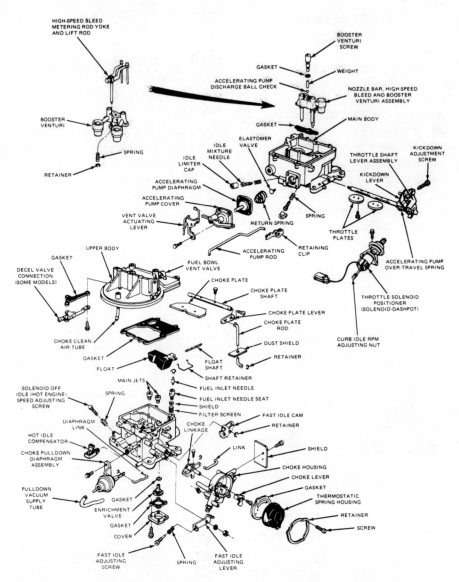

Fig. 29   2150 carburetor exploded

2100, 2150 CARBURETOR ADJUSTMENTS

Dry Float Level

With the air horn removed, float raised and the fuel inlet needle seated, measure the distance between the top surface of the throttle body and the top surface of the float. The measurement should be taken near the center of the float at a point about ⅛″ from the free end of the float.

If a cardboard gauge is being used, place the gauge in the corner of the enlarged end section of the fuel bowl as shown in Fig. 30. The gauge should touch the float near the end but not on the end radius.

Depress the float tab to seat the fuel inlet needle. The float height is measured from the gasket surface of the throttle body, with the gasket removed. If the measurement is not as

listed in the chart, bend the tab as required to obtain the correct setting.

Wet Float Level

With the car on a level surface, run the engine until normal operating temperature is reached. Then shut off the engine and check the fuel level as follows:

1. Remove the air cleaner assembly.
2. Remove the screws securing the carburetor air horn and leave the air horn in place on the carburetor.
3. Start the engine and allow it to idle for a few minutes.
4. Then rotate the air horn and remove its gasket to gain access to float.
5. While engine is idling, measure vertical distance from top

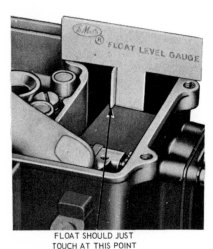

FLOAT SHOULD JUST
TOUCH AT THIS POINT

Fig. 30   2100, 2150 dry float level adjustment

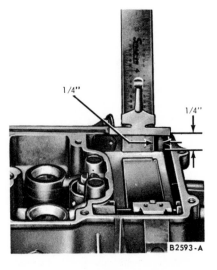

Fig. 31   2100, 2150 wet float level adjustment

Fig. 32   2100, 2150 pump stroke adjustment

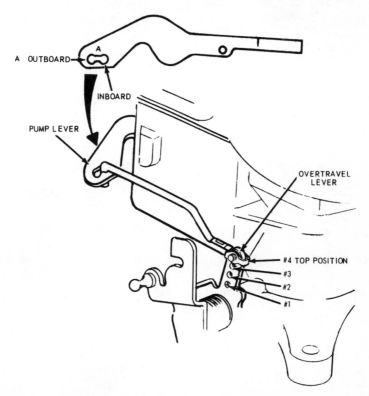

Fig. 33   2100, 2150 pump stroke adjustment

machined surface of throttle body
to the level of the fuel in the bowl.
Make measurement at least ¼"

away from any vertical surface to
assure correct reading, Fig. 31.
6. If level is not as listed in the chart,

51

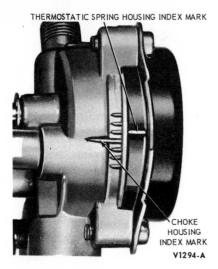

THERMOSTATIC SPRING HOUSING INDEX MARK

CHOKE
HOUSING
INDEX MARK

V1294-A

Fig. 34   2100, 2150 choke setting

and the accelerating pump link may have either 2 or 4 holes to control the pump stroke to compensate for various temperatures, operating conditions and engine applications. The correct pump position, as listed in the chart, should not be changed.

Adjustment is made as follows, Figs. 32 and 33.

1. To release the rod from the retainer clip, press the tab end of the clip toward the rod while at the same time pressing the rod away from the clip until it is disengaged.

2. Position the clip over the specified hole in the throttle shaft lever. Press the ends of the clip together and insert the operating rod through the clip and lever. Release the clip to engage the rod.

stop the engine, and adjust the level by bending the float tab contacting the needle. Bend it upward to raise the fuel level and downward to lower the fuel level.

7. Restart engine and check fuel level.

8. When level is correct, replace carburetor air horn using a new gasket.

Accelerating Pump Adjustment

The throttle shaft lever has 4 holes

Choke Setting

Turn the thermostatic spring cover against spring tension until the index mark on the cover is aligned with the specified mark on the choke housing, Fig. 34.

2100, 2150 CARBURETOR ADJUSTMENT DATA
*Number stamped on tag affixed to carburetor body.

Year	Carb. No.*	Float Level Dry	Fuel Level Wet	Pump Hole No.	Choke Setting
1970	DOAF-C	$7/16$	$13/16$	No. 3	1 Rich
	DOAF-D	$7/16$	$13/16$	No. 3	1 Rich
	DOAF-E	$7/16$	$13/16$	No. 3	2 Lean

2100, 2150 CARBURETOR ADJUSTMENT DATA *(continued)*

*Number stamped on tag affixed to carburetor body.

Year	Carb. No.*	Float Level Dry	Fuel Level Wet	Pump Hole No.	Choke Setting
	DOAF-F	$7/16$	$13/16$	No. 3	2 Lean
	DOAF-J	$7/16$	$13/16$	No. 3	—
	DOAF-T	$7/16$	$13/16$	No. 3	—
	DOAF-U	$7/16$	$13/16$	No. 3	1 Rich
	DOAF-V	$7/16$	$13/16$	No. 3	2 Lean
	DOAF-Y	$7/16$	$13/16$	No. 3	1 Rich
	DOAF-Z	$7/16$	$13/16$	No. 3	—
	DOAF-AA	$7/16$	$13/16$	No. 3	—
1971	DIAF-DA	$7/16$	$13/16$	No. 3	1 Rich
	DIAF-FA	$7/16$	$13/16$	No. 3	1 Rich
	DIAF-JA	$7/16$	$13/16$	No. 3	Index
	DIAF-KA	$7/16$	$13/16$	No. 3	Index
	DIMF-FA	$7/16$	$13/16$	No. 3	1 Rich
	DIMF-JA	$7/16$	$13/16$	No. 3	1 Rich
	DIMF-KA	$7/16$	$13/16$	No. 3	1 Rich
	DIOF-ABA	$7/16$	$13/16$	No. 3	1 Rich
	DIYF-DA	$7/16$	$13/16$	No. 3	Index
	DIZF-AA	$7/16$	$13/16$	No. 2	Index
1972	D2AF-FB	$7/16$	$13/16$	No. 3	Index
	D2AF-GB	$7/16$	$13/16$	No. 3	Index
	D2GF-AA	$7/16$	$13/16$	No. 2	1 Rich
	D2GF-BA	$7/16$	$13/16$	No. 2	1 Rich
	D2MF-FB	$7/16$	$13/16$	No. 4	1 Rich
	D20F-UB	$7/16$	$13/16$	No. 3	①
	D2WF-CA	$7/16$	$13/16$	No. 3	①
1973	D3AF-CE	$7/16$	$13/16$	No. 2	2 Rich
	D3AF-DC	$7/16$	$13/16$	No. 3	3 Rich
	D3AF-KA	$7/16$	$13/16$	No. 3	3 Rich
	D3MF-AE	$7/16$	$13/16$	No. 3	3 Rich
	D3MF-BA	$7/16$	$13/16$	No. 3	3 Rich
1974	D4AE-DA	$7/16$	$13/16$	No. 2A	1 Rich
	D4AE-EA	$7/16$	$13/16$	No. 2A	3 Rich
	D4AE-FA	$7/16$	$13/16$	No. 3A	3 Rich

2100, 2150 CARBURETOR ADJUSTMENT DATA *(continued)*

*Number stamped on tag affixed to carburetor body.

Year	Carb. No.*	Float Level Dry	Fuel Level Wet	Pump Hole No.	Choke Setting
	D4AE-GA	$^7/_{16}$	$^{13}/_{16}$	No. 3A	3 Rich
	D4AE-HB	$^7/_{16}$	$^{13}/_{16}$	No. 3A	3 Rich
	D4ME-BA	$^7/_{16}$	$^{13}/_{16}$	No. 3A	3 Rich
	D4ME-CA	$^7/_{16}$	$^{13}/_{16}$	No. 3A	3 Rich
1975	D5AE-AA	$^7/_{16}$	$^{13}/_{16}$	No. 3	3 Rich
	D5AE-EA	$^7/_{16}$	$^{13}/_{16}$	No. 3	3 Rich
	D5ME-BA	$^7/_{16}$	$^{13}/_{16}$	No. 2	3 Rich
	D5ME-FA	$^7/_{16}$	$^{13}/_{16}$	No. 2	3 Rich
	D5OE-BA	$^7/_{16}$	$^{13}/_{16}$	No. 3	3 Rich
	D5OE-CA	$^7/_{16}$	$^{13}/_{16}$	No. 3	3 Rich
	D5OE-GA	$^7/_{16}$	$^{13}/_{16}$	No. 2	3 Rich
1976	D6AE-HA	$^7/_{16}$	$^{13}/_{16}$	No. 2	3 Rich
	D6ME-AA	$^7/_{16}$	$^{13}/_{16}$	No. 2	3 Rich
	D6WE-AA	$^7/_{16}$	$^{13}/_{16}$	No. 2	3 Rich
	D6WE-BA	$^7/_{16}$	$^{13}/_{16}$	No. 2	2 Rich
1977	D7AE-AHA	$^7/_{16}$	$^{13}/_{16}$	No. 3	Index
	D7AE-ACA	$^7/_{16}$	$^{13}/_{16}$	No. 2	Index
	D7AE-AKA	$^7/_{16}$	$^{13}/_{16}$	No. 3	Index
	D7OE-RA	$^7/_{16}$	$^{13}/_{16}$	No. 3	2 Rich
	D7OE-LA	$^7/_{16}$	$^{13}/_{16}$	No. 4	3 Rich
	D7OE-TA	$^7/_{16}$	$^{13}/_{16}$	No. 3	2 Rich

①—California models, 1 rich; all others, 2 rich.

4300, 4350 CARBURETOR ADJUSTMENTS

Float Level

Referring to Figs. 37 and 38, proceed as follows:

1. Set the gauge to the specified height as listed in the chart.
2. Insert the gauge into the outboard air horn holes as shown.
3. Both floats should just touch the gauge for the proper setting.
4. To adjust floats, bend the primary needle tab downward to raise the float and upward to lower the float.

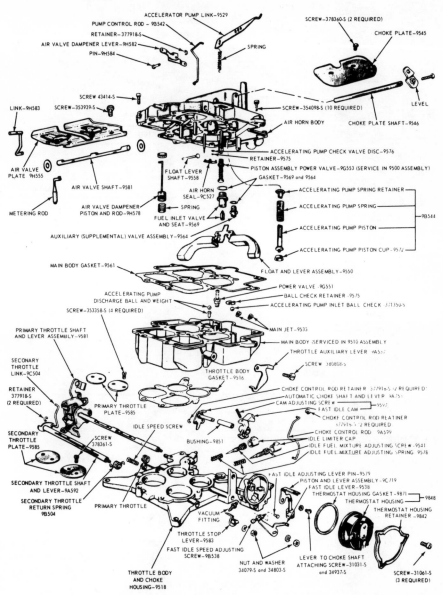

ACCELERATOR PUMP LINK-9529
PUMP CONTROL ROD - 9B542
RETAINER - 377918-S
AIR VALVE DAMPENER LEVER-9H582
PIN-9H584
SPRING

SCREW-378360-S (2 REQUIRED)
CHOKE PLATE-9545

SCREW 43414-S
SCREW-353939-S
LINK-9H583
SCREW-354098-S (10 REQUIRED)
AIR HORN BODY
LEVEL
CHOKE PLATE SHAFT-9546

AIR VALVE
PLATE 9H555
AIR VALVE SHAFT-9581
FLOAT LEVER
SHAFT-9558
AIR HORN
SEAL-9C527
ACCELERATING PUMP CHECK VALVE DISC-9576
RETAINER-9575
PISTON ASSEMBLY POWER VALVE-9G553 (SERVICE IN 9500 ASSEMBLY)
GASKET-9569 and 9564

ACCELERATING PUMP SPRING RETAINER
ACCELERATING PUMP SPRING
METERING ROD
AIR VALVE DAMPENER
PISTON AND ROD-9H578
SPRING
FUEL INLET VALVE
AND SEAT-9569
ACCELERATING PUMP PISTON
9B544
ACCELERATING PUMP PISTON CUP-9572
AUXILIARY (SUPPLEMENTAL) VALVE ASSEMBLY-9564

MAIN BODY GASKET-9561
FLOAT AND LEVER ASSEMBLY-9550
POWER VALVE-9G551
ACCELERATING PUMP
DISCHARGE BALL AND WEIGHT
SCREW-353358-S (4 REQUIRED)
BALL CHECK RETAINER-9575
ACCELERATING PUMP INLET BALL CHECK-371350-S

PRIMARY THROTTLE SHAFT
AND LEVER ASSEMBLY-9581
MAIN JET-9533
MAIN BODY (SERVICED IN 9510 ASSEMBLY)
THROTTLE AUXILIARY LEVER-9A537
SECONARY
THROTTLE
LINK-9C504
THROTTLE BODY
GASKET-9516
SCREW 380808-S

RETAINER
377918-S
(2 REQUIRED)
PRIMARY THROTTLE
PLATE-9585
CHOKE CONTROL ROD RETAINER-377918-S (2 REQUIRED)
AUTOMATIC CHOKE SHAFT AND LEVER-9A753
CAM ADJUSTING SCREW
9597
FAST IDLE CAM
CHOKE CONTROL ROD RETAINER
377918-S (2 REQUIRED)
SECONDARY
THROTTLE
PLATE-9585
IDLE SPEED SCREW
SCREW
378361-S
BUSHING-9851
CHOKE CONTROL ROD-9A599
IDLE LIMITER CAP
IDLE FUEL MIXTURE ADJUSTING SCREW-9541
IDLE FUEL MIXTURE ADJUSTING SPRING 9576

SECONDARY THROTTLE SHAFT
AND LEVER-9A592
SECONDARY THROTTLE
RETURN SPRING
9B504
PRIMARY THROTTLE
FAST IDLE ADJUSTING LEVER PIN-9579
PISTON AND LEVER ASSEMBLY-9C719
FAST IDLE LEVER-9538
THERMOSTAT HOUSING GASKET-9871
THERMOSTAT HOUSING
9848
THERMOSTAT HOUSING
RETAINER-9842

VACUUM
FITTING
THROTTLE STOP
LEVER-9583
FAST IDLE SPEED ADJUSTING
SCREW-9B538
NUT AND WASHER
34079-S and 34803-S
LEVER TO CHOKE SHAFT
ATTACHING SCREW-31031-S
and 34937-S
SCREW-31061-S
(3 REQUIRED)
THROTTLE BODY
AND CHOKE
HOUSING-9518

Fig. 35   4300 carburetor exploded

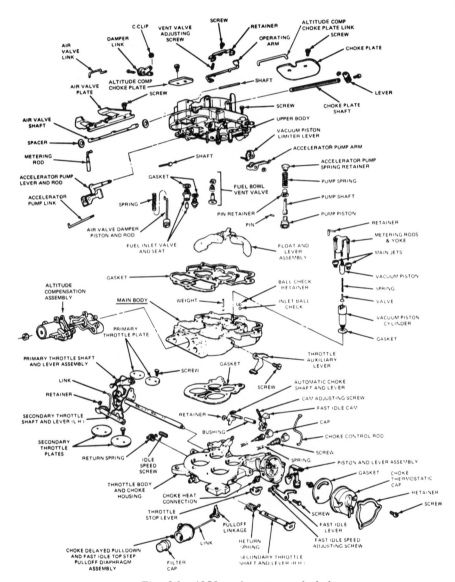

Fig. 36   4350 carburetor exploded

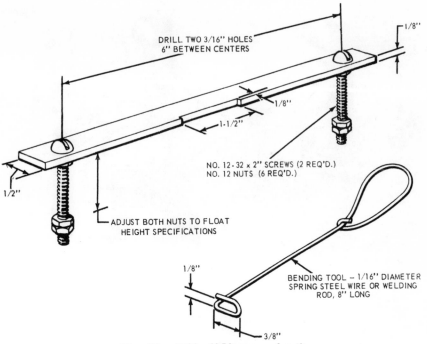

DRILL TWO 3/16'' HOLES
6'' BETWEEN CENTERS

1/8''

1/8''

1-1/2''

NO. 12-32 x 2'' SCREWS (2 REQ'D.)
NO. 12 NUTS (6 REQ'D.)

1/2''

ADJUST BOTH NUTS TO FLOAT
HEIGHT SPECIFICATIONS

1/8''

BENDING TOOL — 1/16'' DIAMETER
SPRING STEEL WIRE OR WELDING
ROD, 8'' LONG

3/8''

Fig. 37   4300, 4350 gauge details

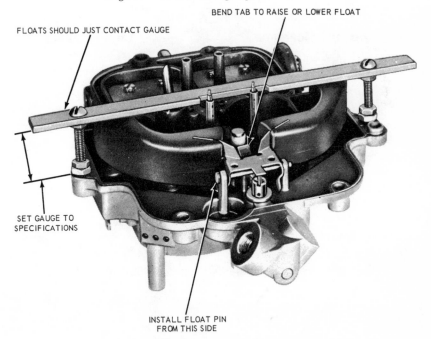

BEND TAB TO RAISE OR LOWER FLOAT

FLOATS SHOULD JUST CONTACT GAUGE

SET GAUGE TO
SPECIFICATIONS

INSTALL FLOAT PIN
FROM THIS SIDE

Fig. 38   4300, 4350 float level adjustment

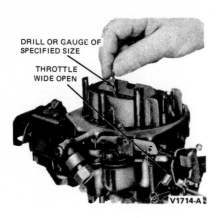

Fig. 39   4300 dechoke clearance

Fig. 40   4300, 4350 choke setting

Accelerating Pump Stroke

The accelerating pump linkage should be in the specified hole as listed in the chart.

Dechoke Clearance

Refer to Fig. 39 and proceed as follows:

1. Open and hold throttle plate in the wide open position.
2. Rotate the choke plate towards the closed position until the pawl on the fast idle speed lever contacts the fast idle cam.
3. Check the clearance between the lower edge of the choke plate and the air horn wall.
4. Adjust to specified setting by bending pawl on fast idle speed lever forward to increase or backward to decrease the clearance.

Choke Setting

Refer to Fig. 40 and proceed as follows:

1. Loosen the choke heat tube nut.
2. Loosen the choke cover retaining screws.
3. Rotate the choke cover clockwise to reduce choking action or counterclockwise to increase choking action and to the setting as listed in the chart.
4. Tighten choke cover screws and choke heat tube nut when desired setting is reached.

4300, 4350 CARBURETOR ADJUSTMENT DATA
*Number stamped on tag affixed to carburetor body

Year	Carb. No.*	Float Level	Pump Hole No.	Choke Pulldown	Choke Setting
1970	DOAF-L	25/32	No. 2	.250	Index
	DOAF-AB	25/32	No. 2	.250	Index
	DOAF-AG	25/32	No. 2	.220	Index
	DOAF-AL	25/32	No. 2	.250	Index
	DOAF-AM	25/32	No. 2	.220	Index
1971	D1AF-MA	49/64	No. 2	.220	Index
1972	D2AF-AA	49/64	No. 1	.220	2 Rich
	D2AF-LA	49/64	No. 1	.215	Index
	D2SF-BA	49/64	No. 1	.220	2 Rich
1973	D3AF-EB	7/8	No. 1	.200	Index
	D3AF-HA	3/4	No. 1	.210	Index
	D3VF-DA	3/4	No. 1	.210	Index
1974	D4AE-AA	3/4	No. 1	.230	Index
	D4AE-NA	3/4	No. 1	.220	Index
	D4VE-AB	3/4	No. 1	.220	Index
1975	D5AE-CA	31/32	No. 1	①	2 Rich
	D5AE-DA	31/32	No. 1	①	2 Rich
	D5VE-AD	15/16	No. 1	①	2 Rich
	D5VE-BA	15/16	No. 1	①	2 Rich
1976	D6AE-CA	1.00	No. 2	②	2 Rich
	D6AE-DA	.960	No. 2	③	2 Rich
1977	D7VE-SA	1.00	No. 2	②	Index

①—Initial setting, .160". Delayed, .190".
②—Initial setting, .140". Delayed, .190."
③—Initial setting, .160; Delayed, .210".

TQ CARBURETOR ADJUSTMENTS

Float Setting

With the bowl cover held upside down, Fig. 42, and the gasket installed and floats resting on the seated needle, the dimension of each float from the bowl cover gasket to the bottom side of the float should be as listed in the chart.

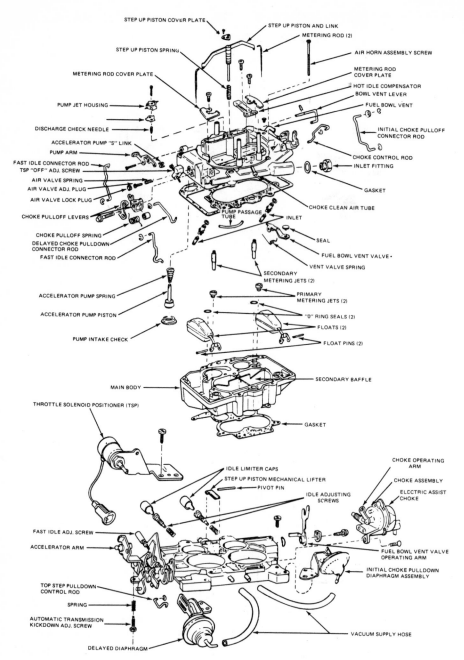

STEP UP PISTON COVER PLATE
STEP UP PISTON AND LINK
METERING ROD (2)
STEP UP PISTON SPRING
AIR HORN ASSEMBLY SCREW
METERING ROD COVER PLATE
METERING ROD COVER PLATE
HOT IDLE COMPENSATOR
BOWL VENT LEVER
PUMP JET HOUSING
FUEL BOWL VENT
DISCHARGE CHECK NEEDLE
INITIAL CHOKE PULLOFF CONNECTOR ROD
ACCELERATOR PUMP "S" LINK
PUMP ARM
CHOKE CONTROL ROD
FAST IDLE CONNECTOR ROD
TSP "OFF" ADJ. SCREW
INLET FITTING
AIR VALVE SPRING
AIR VALVE ADJ. PLUG
GASKET
AIR VALVE LOCK PLUG
CHOKE CLEAN AIR TUBE
CHOKE PULLOFF LEVERS
PUMP PASSAGE TUBE
INLET
CHOKE PULLOFF SPRING
SEAL
DELAYED CHOKE PULLDOWN CONNECTOR ROD
FUEL BOWL VENT VALVE
FAST IDLE CONNECTOR ROD
VENT VALVE SPRING
SECONDARY METERING JETS (2)
ACCELERATOR PUMP SPRING
PRIMARY METERING JETS (2)
ACCELERATOR PUMP PISTON
"O" RING SEALS (2)
FLOATS (2)
PUMP INTAKE CHECK
FLOAT PINS (2)
SECONDARY BAFFLE
MAIN BODY
THROTTLE SOLENOID POSITIONER (TSP)
GASKET
CHOKE OPERATING ARM
IDLE LIMITER CAPS
STEP UP PISTON MECHANICAL LIFTER
CHOKE ASSEMBLY
PIVOT PIN
ELECTRIC ASSIST CHOKE
IDLE ADJUSTING SCREWS
FAST IDLE ADJ. SCREW
ACCELERATOR ARM
FUEL BOWL VENT VALVE OPERATING ARM
INITIAL CHOKE PULLDOWN DIAPHRAGM ASSEMBLY
TOP STEP PULLDOWN CONTROL ROD
SPRING
AUTOMATIC TRANSMISSION KICKDOWN ADJ. SCREW
VACUUM SUPPLY HOSE
DELAYED DIAPHRAGM

Fig. 41   TQ carburetor exploded

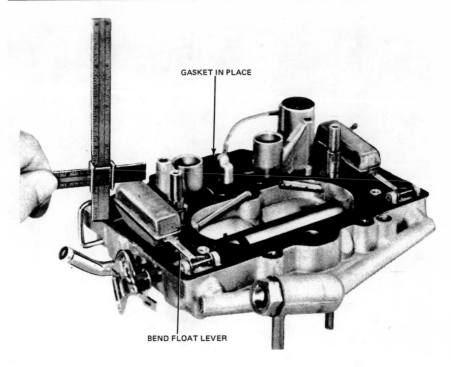

GASKET IN PLACE

BEND FLOAT LEVER

Fig. 42   TQ float setting

Pump Travel

Move the choke valve to the wide open position to release the fast idle cam. Back off the idle speed adjusting screw until the throttle valves are seated in their bores. Be sure the throttle connector rod is in the center hole of the pump arm. Close the throttle valve tightly and measure the distance between the top of the bowl cover and the end of the plunger shaft. Bend the throttle connector rod at the lower angle to adjust, Fig. 43.

Choke Unloader

Referring to Fig. 44, hold the throttle valves in the wide open position and insert a drill of the specified dimension as listed in the chart, the lower edge of the choke valve and the inner wall of the air horn. With finger pressure on the choke valve control lever, a slight drag should be felt as the drill is withdrawn. Bend the tang on the fast idle control lever to adjust.

Choke Setting

Loosen the choke cover retaining screws and rotate the cover until the line or index mark on the cover aligns with the proper mark on the housing as listed in the chart.

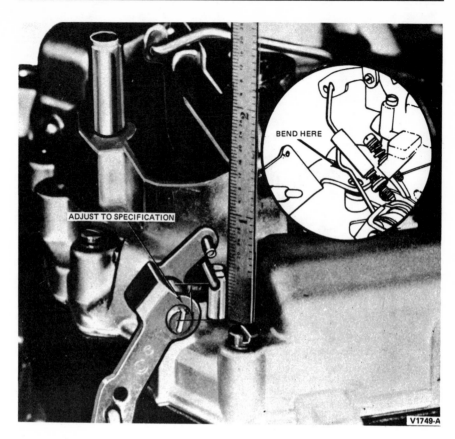

Fig. 43   TQ pump travel

TQ CARBURETOR ADJUSTMENT DATA
*Number stamped on tag affixed to carburetor body

Year	Carb. No.*	Float Setting	Pump Travel	Choke Unloader	Choke Setting
1974	D4AE-BC	$1^1/_{16}$	$^5/_{16}$	.250	Index

FUEL PUMP PRESSURE

Fuel pressure is measured with a gauge capable of measuring vacuum and fuel pump pressure. If you can get access to such a gauge, here's how you use it.

1. At the fuel pump, disconnect the fuel line leading to the carburetor.

2. Attach the pressure gauge to the

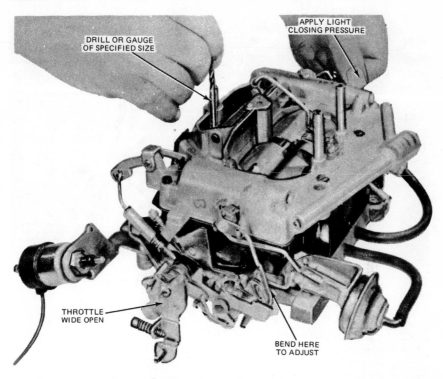

Fig. 44   TQ choke unloader

port from which the line was disconnected.

3. Using the ignition key, turn it to the Start position and crank the engine through a few revolutions and observe the reading on the gauge. If the reading does not meet the specification as listed below in the chart, the fuel pump has probably failed. A low reading can be cause for poor engine performance at high speed. Generally, when a pump has failed, the engine will not start or will stall a short while after starting and consuming the fuel that remains in the carburetor bowl.

Year	Engine	Pressure Lbs.
1970–72	6–240	4–6
1970–71	V8 exc. 302	5–7
1970–71	V8–302	4–6
1972–75	V8 exc. 1974–75 460	5–7
1974	V8-460 Calif.	5.7–7.7
1974	V8-460 exc. Calif.	5–7
1976	V8-350, 400	6–8
1975–77	V8-460	5.7–7.7
1977	V8-351, 400	6–8

FUEL PUMP REPLACEMENT

Before removing the fuel pump, rotate the engine so that the low point of the fuel pump cam lobe is against the pump arm. This can be determined by rotating the engine slowly with the pump held loosely in position until the tension is removed from the arm. To replace the pump, proceed as follows:

1. Disconnect the fuel lines from the pump. Plug the line coming to the pump from the tank so fuel will not drain.
2. Remove the pump attaching bolts

and remove the pump and gasket. Be sure all traces of the old gasket are removed from the pump and the engine.
3. Install the replacement pump and a new gasket.
4. Connect the fuel lines to the pump and start the engine to check for leaks. Do not neglect to examine the fuel pump flex line at this time as it may require replacing.

Emission Controls

Due to the complex nature of the many and varied units used to eliminate air pollution and contribute to good driveability, we will confine our coverage in this chapter to only the very simple systems on which you can easily perform routine maintenance.

not stuck. If you do not hear this click the valve is stuck and should be replaced. Do not attempt to clean this valve. It must be replaced when stuck.
2. Be sure to check the hoses leading to the valve to be sure they are clean.

POSITIVE CRANKCASE VENTILATION VALVE (PCV)

Refer to Figs. 45 and 46 for the location of the positive crankcase ventilation valve on the various six cylinder and V8 engines. Remove the valve from the hose or breather oil filler cap and check it to see if it is stuck, as follows:

1. While holding the valve in your fingers, turn it upside down. You should hear a click if the valve is

CRANKCASE VENTILATION FILTER REPLACEMENT

The crankcase ventilation filter is found inside the air cleaner body secured to the rim. A clip is used outside the body of the air cleaner to retain the neck of the ventilation filter. Refer to Figs. 47 and 48 and proceed as follows:

1. Remove the top lid of the air cleaner after removing the wing nut.

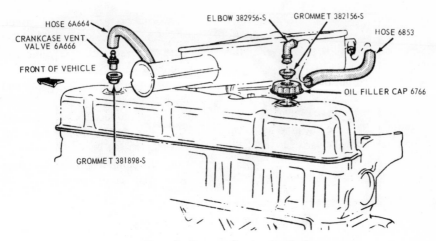

Fig. 45   Six cylinder crankcase ventilation system

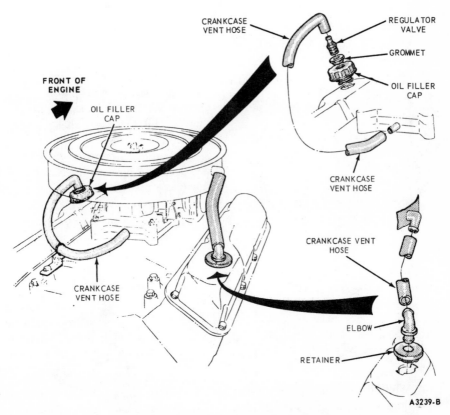

Fig. 46   V8 crankcase ventilation system

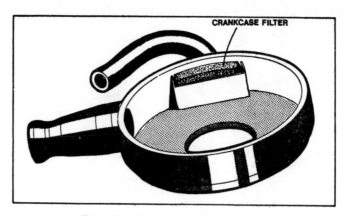

Fig. 47   Ventilation filter location

OIL FILLER BREATHER CAP

2. Locate the ventilation filter at the inside rim of the air cleaner and remove the clip from the neck of the filter. Remove the hose attached to the neck.
3. Lift out the old filter pack and install the new filter.
4. Replace the retaining clip and install the hose on the neck.

Periodically, the oil filler breather cap should be removed and cleaned. If the cap has a hose attached to it, remove the hose and PCV valve and lift the cap from the rocker arm cover. Agitate the cap in mineral spirits to clean the filter element. Shake the cap dry, do not dry the cap with air pressure. Reinstall the cap on the engine and attach the hose and PCV valve, if previously removed.

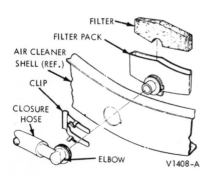

Fig. 48   Ventilation filter details

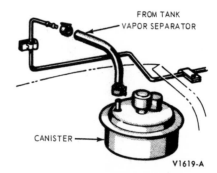

Fig. 49   Fuel evaporative emission canister

FUEL EVAPORATIVE EMISSION CANISTER

This canister should be replaced at recommended intervals as shown in the maintenance charts at the front of this book. The canister is located to one side of the radiator on either the right or left side, Fig. 49. Simply tag and disconnect the hoses and remove the canister from the bracket. Replace the canister with a new one and reinstall the hoses previously removed.

Electrical

JUMP STARTING A CAR WITH A DEAD BATTERY

Before attempting any jump start, be sure the booster cables you are using are heavy duty cables with good insulation on the clamps and cables. Good quality booster cables, using at least a number 6 or 8 gauge wire for stranding, are essential. Cables of insufficient wire gauge will quickly dissipate the voltage from the good battery and have very little left to provide a jump start. Also, you may risk personal injury, using cables or clamps improperly insulated. If the clamps get hot during the jump start operation, it is likely the booster cables are not adequate.

Whenever your car battery is dead, it is important that the battery being used to jump start it is of the same voltage and that it also be a negative ground battery. *Do not allow the cars to touch while attempting to jump start.*

Connect the cables as follows:

1. Connect one end of one cable (red positive) to the positive terminal of the dead battery, Fig. 50.

2. Connect the other end of this same cable to the positive terminal of the good battery.
3. Start the car with the good battery and allow it to run at fast idle for a few minutes.
4. Now connect one end of the remaining cable to the negative terminal of the good battery and then clamp the remaining end of the cable to a good ground on the engine with the dead battery.
5. Start the engine with the dead battery and allow it to run at fast idle for a few minutes.
6. Remove the cable end clamped to ground and then remove the other end of this cable from the negative terminal of the car with the good battery.
7. Now remove the remaining cable from both cars.
8. Have the dead battery tested as soon as possible as it may no longer be serviceable in which case it will only go dead again. Also, there may be charging system problems which should be diagnosed by a skilled mechanic using proper equipment.

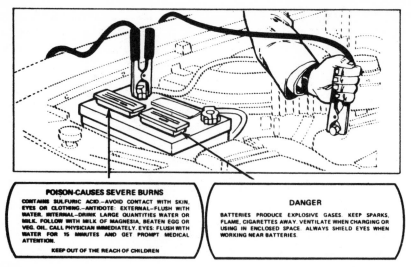

POISON-CAUSES SEVERE BURNS

CONTAINS SULFURIC ACID.—AVOID CONTACT WITH SKIN, EYES OR CLOTHING.—ANTIDOTE: EXTERNAL—FLUSH WITH WATER. INTERNAL—DRINK LARGE QUANTITIES WATER OR MILK. FOLLOW WITH MILK OF MAGNESIA, BEATEN EGG OR VEG. OIL. CALL PHYSICIAN IMMEDIATELY. EYES: FLUSH WITH WATER FOR 15 MINUTES AND GET PROMPT MEDICAL ATTENTION.

KEEP OUT OF THE REACH OF CHILDREN

DANGER

BATTERIES PRODUCE EXPLOSIVE GASES. KEEP SPARKS, FLAME, CIGARETTES AWAY. VENTILATE WHEN CHARGING OR USING IN ENCLOSED SPACE. ALWAYS SHIELD EYES WHEN WORKING NEAR BATTERIES.

Fig. 50   Attaching booster cables. Notice that negative cable is attached to a good engine ground

BATTERY & CABLE CARE

Too often the cause of a dead battery or a no start complaint can be directly traced to a build-up of acid corrosion on the battery terminals which allows the battery voltage to leak to ground and slowly discharge the battery or to broken or frayed battery cables. In cold weather, if the battery charge is not maintained and cells kept filled it is likely the battery will freeze or at least not provide enough voltage to start the car.

Examine the battery periodically to be sure the cells are filled and that acid build-up is removed, Fig. 51. A sim-

Fig. 51   Cleaning battery posts

Fig. 52   Inspect battery cables

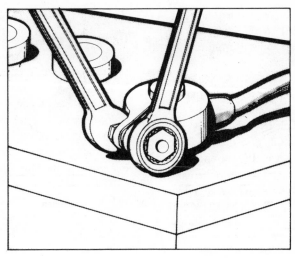

Fig. 53   Tighten battery cables

ple solution of water and baking soda will remove the acid build-up from the cables and battery terminals. Do not allow this solution to enter the battery cells. The easiest way to perform this service is to remove the battery from the car. Now the battery tray can be cleaned of all acid traces as well as the cable ends. Examine the cable terminals closely for broken or frayed strands or insulation, Fig. 52. Replace any cables showing these signs. Remove the caps from the battery and fill the cells with water. Distilled water should be used if the mineral content of local water is high. Replace the caps and wipe the battery clean and reinstall it in the car. Coat the battery terminals lightly with petrolatum after replacing and tightening the cables, Fig. 53. Be sure cables are replaced on the correct terminals. The negative (−) terminal of the battery goes to ground and it should always be connected last and removed first to avoid sparks.

ALTERNATOR REPLACEMENT

If your dead battery is being caused by a no charge condition, the alternator is most likely the cause. You can save the expense involved in the removal and overhaul of this unit simply by removing it yourself and replacing it with a new or rebuilt unit which can be obtained at your local auto parts supply store. You can also check with your local salvage yard. Although the cars these parts came from were wrecked, they may well be in good condition and have many thousands of miles left in them. Be sure you fully understand any warranty that you may get with all new, used or rebuilt parts.

Here's how to remove the alternator.

1. Disconnect the battery ground cable to prevent accidental shorts.
2. Loosen the alternator mounting bolts and remove the attaching

bolt from the adjustment arm.
3. Slip the belt off the pulleys.
4. Properly tag and remove the wires from the alternator.
5. Now remove the alternator mounting bolt and remove the alternator.
6. Install the new alternator and slip the drive belt over the pulleys.
7. Using a length of wood, pry the alternator away from the engine to properly tension the drive belt and tighten the alternator bolts. When prying, use a piece of wood placed against the alternator housing to pry against so as not to damage the alternator.
8. Reconnect the alternator wires to their terminals and start the engine to check that the alternator is charging.

STARTER MOTOR REPLACEMENT

A slow cranking complaint can be caused by the starter motor having too much resistance. In other words, the battery voltage is being used up in trying to activate the starter motor and too little is left to crank the engine. This symptom calls for removal and subsequent overhaul of the starter. You can remove the starter yourself and replace it with a new or rebuilt unit which you can purchase at your local auto parts supply store. And, once again, don't forget the auto salvage yard. You can get one here at a greatly reduced price and save the costly overhaul. Furthermore, you will also have replaced the solenoid and the starter drive.

Remove the starter motor as follows:

1. Disconnect the battery ground cable to prevent accidental shorts.
2. Disconnect the starter cable from the starter terminal.
3. Remove the starter mounting bolts and remove the starter assembly. It may be necessary on some models to turn the steering wheel to the extreme left or right or perhaps even to disconnect and lower the idler arm from the frame to gain access to remove the starter.

RADIO REMOVAL

If your radio has been blowing fuses, the chances are it must come out for repair. You can save a big part of the total repair cost by removing the radio yourself and taking it to the radio repair shop. Since the radio and television repair men are not auto mechanics, you can remove the radio just as easily as they can and here is how to do it.

1970

1. Disconnect the battery ground cable to avoid accidental shorts.
2. Remove the radio, windshield wiper and windshield washer control knobs.
3. Remove the lighter element and pull off the heater switch knobs.
4. Remove the ten screws retaining the instrument panel trim cover and remove the assembly.

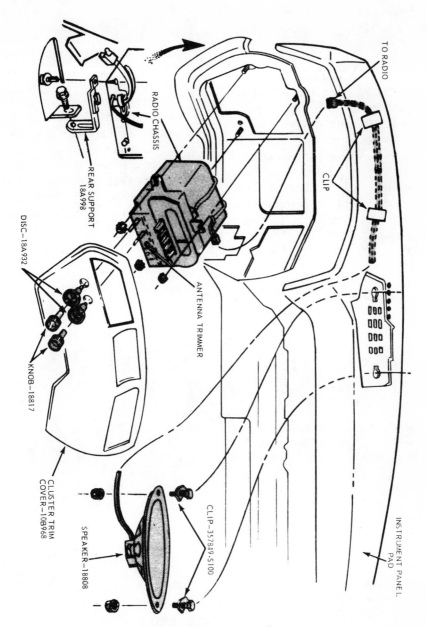

TO RADIO

RADIO CHASSIS

REAR SUPPORT
18A998

CLIP

DISC–18A932

ANTENNA TRIMMER

KNOB–18817

CLUSTER TRIM
COVER–10B968

SPEAKER–18808

CLIP–357849-S100

INSTRUMENT PANEL
PAD

Fig. 54   Radio removal. 1970

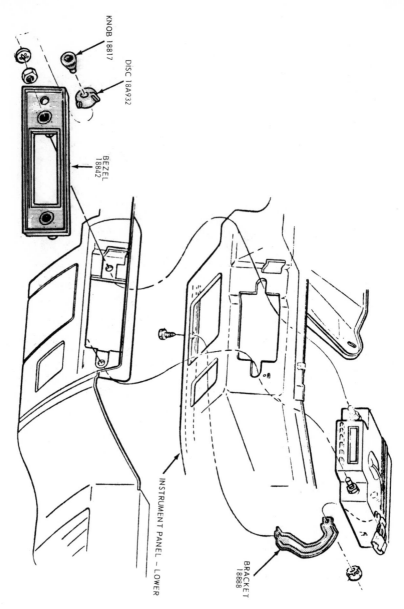

KNOB 18817

DISC 18A932

BEZEL 18842

INSTRUMENT PANEL – LOWER

BRACKET 18888

Fig. 55   Radio removal. 1971-72

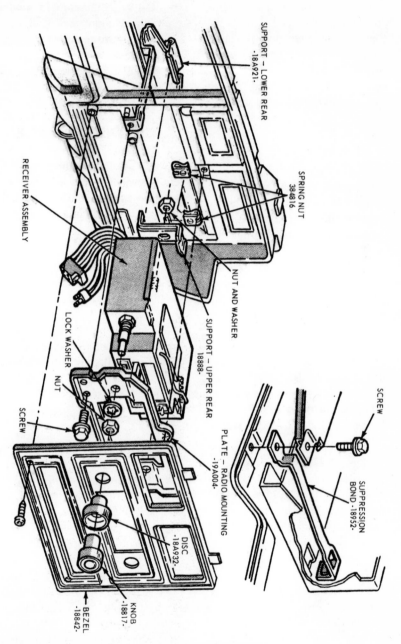

Fig. 56   Radio removal. 1973-77

5. Remove the lower rear radio support bolts, fig. 54.
6. Remove the three nuts retaining the radio to the instrument panel and pull the radio part way out.
7. Disconnect the speaker, power and antenna leads and remove radio.

1971–72

1. Disconnect the battery ground cable to prevent accidental shorts.
2. Remove the radio knobs and remove the two nuts retaining the bezel to the radio, Fig. 55.
3. Remove the radio bezel and the nut retaining the fader control to the bezel.
4. Remove the rear radio support attaching screw and nut and remove the support.
5. Disconnect the power, speaker and antenna leads.
6. Remove the two nuts and washers retaining the radio to the instrument panel and remove the radio.

1973–77

1. Disconnect the battery ground cable to prevent accidental shorts.
2. Remove the radio knobs and the screws attaching the bezel to the instrument panel and then remove the bezel, Fig. 56.
3. Remove the radio mounting plate attaching screws.
4. Pull the radio to disengage it from the lower rear support bracket.
5. Disconnect the power, speaker and antenna leads and remove the radio.

6. Remove the radio to mounting plate retaining nuts and washers and remove the mounting plate.
7. Remove the rear upper support retaining nut and remove the support.

W/S WIPER BLADES

There are two methods used to retain the wiper blades and they are referred to as the bayonet type and the pin type, Figs. 57 and 58.

Bayonet Type: To remove a Trico manufactured blade, press down on the arm to unlock the top stud, depress the tab on the saddle and pull the blade from the arm. To remove an Anco manufactured blade, press inward on the tab and pull the blade from the arm. To install a new blade assembly, slide the blade saddle over the end of the wiper arm so that the locking stud snaps into place.

Side Saddle Pin Type: To remove the pin type, insert the screwdriver into the spring release opening of the blade saddle and depress the spring clip and pull the blade from the arm. To install, push the blade saddle onto the pin so that the spring clip engages pin. To replace the rubber element in a Trico blade, squeeze the latch lock release and pull the element out of the lever jaws, Fig. 59. Remove the Anco element by depressing the latch pin and sliding the element out of the yoke jaws. To install the element, insert it through the yoke or lever jaws making sure it is fully engaged at all points.

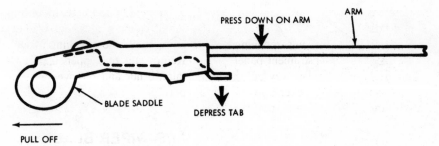

Fig. 57   Trico bayonet type blade removal

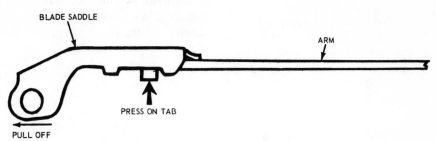

Fig. 58   Anco bayonet type blade removal

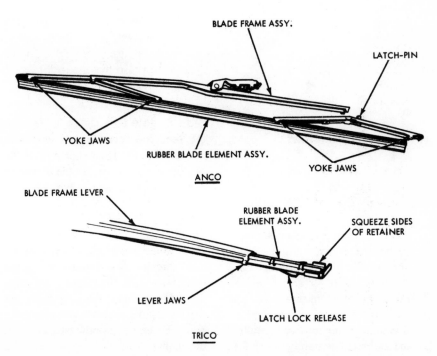

Fig. 59   Rubber wiper element replacement

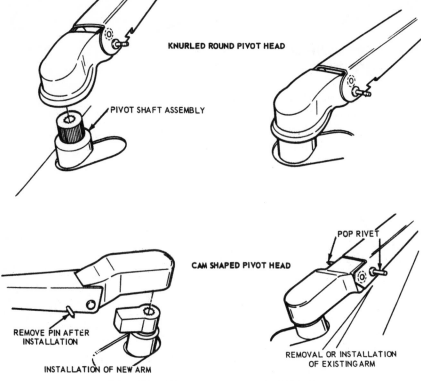

Fig. 60   Wiper arm removal. 1970-72

W/S WIPER ARMS

1970–72

1. Swing the arm and blade assembly away from the windshield and insert a $^3/_{32}''$ pin or drill through the pin hole as shown in Fig. 60. This will release the spring loaded attaching clip in the arm from the pivot shaft and inserting the pin will hold it in the released position. The arm can now be pulled off the pivot shaft.
2. The driver's side auxiliary arm is removed after the driver's side wiper arm. Then slide the retaining clip back and lift the arm from the pin as shown in Fig. 61.

1973–77

Raise the blade end of the arm off the windshield and move the slide latch away from the pivot shaft, Fig. 62. This unlocks the arm from the shaft and holds the blade end off the glass. The arm can now be pulled off the shaft.

The auxiliary arm on the driver's

side is held on the pin by the shoulder of the main arm.

W/S WIPER TRANSMISSION

1. Disconnect the battery ground cable to prevent accidental shorts.
2. Remove the windshield wiper arm and blade assemblies from the pivot shafts.'
3. Remove the cowl screens for access to the linkage.
4. Disconnect the left linkage arm from the drive arm by removing the clip.
5. Then remove the three bolts retaining the left pivot shaft assembly to the cowl and remove the left arm and pivot shaft through the cowl opening.
6. Disconnect the linkage drive arm from the motor crank pin by removing the clip, Fig. 63.
7. Remove the three bolts that connect the drive arm pivot shaft assembly to the cowl and remove the pivot shaft drive arm and right arm as an assembly.

W/S WIPER MOTOR REPLACEMENT

If the wiper motor stops working, check the fuse and if it is blown, replace it with another one of the same size and amperage. If this fuse also blows, a short is indicated which may be caused by a chafed wire, bad switch or a bad motor. You can remove the wiper motor yourself and save the labor charge. Here is how to do it.

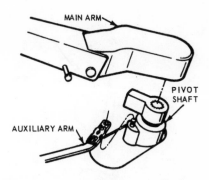

Fig. 61   Auxiliary arm installation. 1970-72

1. Disconnect the battery ground cable to prevent accidental shorts.
2. Remove the wiper arm and blade assemblies from the pivot shafts.
3. Remove the left cowl screen for access through the cowl opening.
4. Disconnect the linkage drive arm from the motor output arm crank pin by removing the retaining clip, Fig. 63.
5. Disconnect the wire connector from the motor.
6. Remove the three bolts retaining the motor to the dash and remove the motor. If the output arm catches on the dash during removal, hand turn the arm clockwise so it will clear the opening in the dash. Before installing the motor, be sure the output arm is in Park position.

W/S WIPER SWITCH REPLACEMENT

1. Disconnect the battery ground cable to prevent accidental shorts.
2. Remove the wiper and headlight switch control knobs.

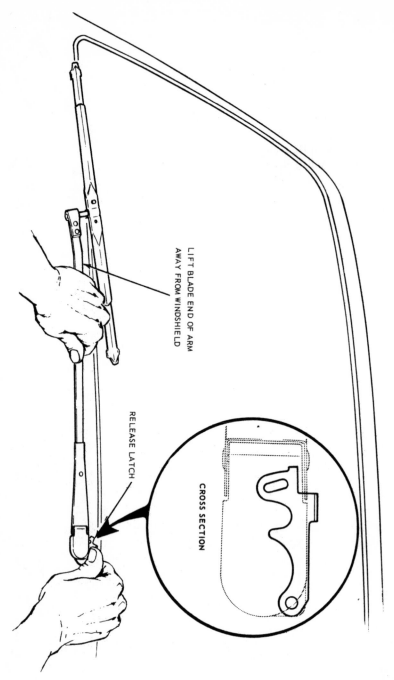

LIFT BLADE END OF ARM
AWAY FROM WINDSHIELD

RELEASE LATCH

CROSS SECTION

Fig. 62   Wiper arm removal. 1973-77

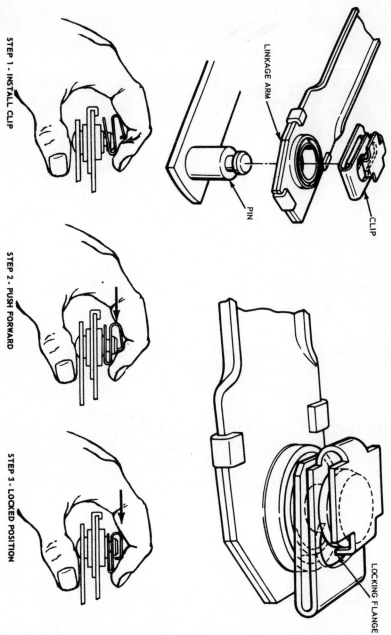

STEP 1 - INSTALL CLIP

STEP 2 - PUSH FORWARD

STEP 3 - LOCKED POSITION

LINKAGE ARM

PIN

CLIP

LOCKING FLANGE

Fig. 63   Installation of wiper arm connecting clip

KNOB RELEASE BUTTON

Fig. 64   Light switch shaft release
button

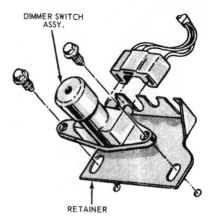

DIMMER SWITCH
ASSY.

RETAINER

Fig. 65   Dimmer switch replacement

3. Remove the headlight switch bezel.
4. Remove the trim panel retaining screw and remove the panel.
5. Remove the wiper switch retaining screws and pull the switch rearward.
6. Disconnect the wiring connector at the switch and remove the switch.

HEADLIGHT SWITCH REPLACEMENT

It may be necessary for you to remove the headlight switch in order to get at something else or to replace the switch itself. Here's how you can do it and save money.

1. To avoid accidental shorts, disconnect the battery ground cable.
2. Pull the control knob to the full On position.
3. Reach up under the instrument panel and depress the shaft release button found on the switch, Fig. 64.

4. While holding the button in, pull the switch knob and shaft out of the switch.
5. Then unscrew the bezel retainer nut from the front of the dash and lower the switch under the panel.
6. Disconnect the switch wiring and remove the switch.

DIMMER SWITCH REPLACEMENT

Pull the floor carpet back from around the area of the switch and remove the mounting screws. It may be necessary to loosen the scuff plate and remove the left cowl trim panel in order to free the carpet. Then disconnect the wiring connector from the switch, Fig. 65 and remove the switch.

STOP LIGHT SWITCH REPLACEMENT

This mechanical switch is installed

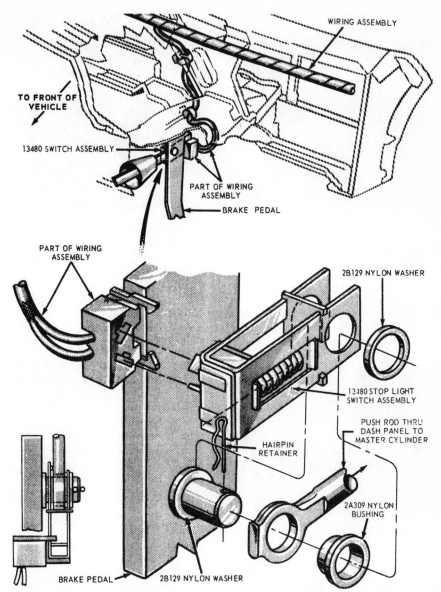

Fig. 66   Stop light switch installation

under the instrument panel on the pin of the brake pedal arm so that it straddles the master cylinder push rod.

1. Reaching up under the instrument panel, disconnect the wires at the connector on the switch, Fig. 66.

2. Remove the hairpin retainer and slide the stoplight switch, the push

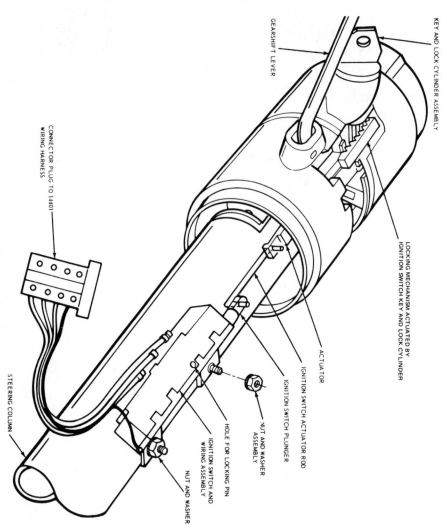

GEARSHIFT LEVER

KEY AND LOCK CYLINDER ASSEMBLY

CONNECTOR PLUG TO 14401
WIRING HARNESS

LOCKING MECHANISM ACTUATED BY
IGNITION SWITCH KEY AND LOCK CYLINDER

STEERING COLUMN

ACTUATOR

IGNITION SWITCH ACTUATOR ROD

IGNITION SWITCH PLUNGER

NUT AND WASHER
ASSEMBLY

HOLE FOR LOCKING PIN

IGNITION SWITCH AND
WIRING ASSEMBLY

NUT AND WASHER

Fig. 67   Pin type ignition switch removal

rod and the nylon washers and bushing away from the brake pedal and remove the switch.

IGNITION SWITCH REPLACEMENT

The ignition switch is located up under the instrument panel mounted on top of the steering column. To get at the switch, remove the steering column shroud and proceed as follows:

Pin Type Connector

1. Detach and lower the steering column from the brake support

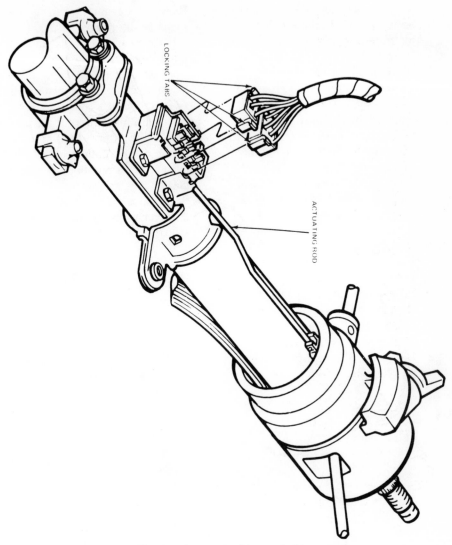

LOCKING TABS

ACTUATING ROD

Fig. 68   Spade type ignition switch removal

bracket.

2. Disconnect the battery ground cable to avoid accidental shorts.

3. Disconnect the switch wiring at the connector, Fig. 67.

4. Remove the two nuts that retain the switch to the steering column.

5. On cars with a column mounted shift lever, detach the switch plunger from the actuator rod and remove the switch.

6. On cars with a floor mounted shift

lever, remove the pin that connects the switch plunger directly to the actuator and remove the switch.

7. When installing the replacement switch, both the locking mechanism at the top of the column and the switch itself must be in the Lock position for correct adjustment. New switches are supplied with a plastic pin installed to hold the switch in the Lock position. After installation of the switch, remove the pin.

Spade Type Connector

1. Disconnect the battery ground cable to prevent accidental shorts.
2. Detach and lower the steering column from the brake support bracket.
3. Disconnect the switch wiring at the plug on the switch, Fig. 68.

4. Remove the nuts securing the switch to the column.
5. Lift the switch vertically upward to disconnect the actuator rod from the switch.
6. When installing the replacement switch, both the locking mechanism at the top of the column and the switch itself must be in the Lock position. Replacement switches are supplied with a plastic pin inserted to hold the switch in the Lock position and this pin must be removed after the switch is installed.

BLOWER MOTOR REPLACEMENT

Models Without Air Conditioning 1970

1. Scribe location marks on the right hood, hinge and mounting panel

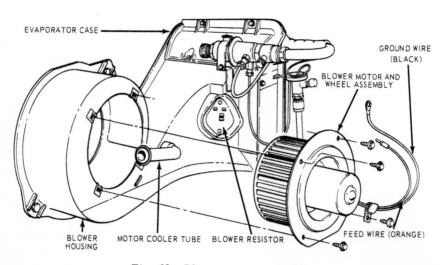

Fig. 69 Blower motor assembly

and remove the hood and right hood hinge.

2. Disconnect the right fender from the fender apron, cowl side panel and front end sheet metal and remove the fender.

3. Disconnect the blower motor wires.

4. Remove the blower motor mounting screws and remove the motor and wheel assembly.

1971–72

1. Remove the battery.

2. Disconnect the blower motor wires.

3. Raise the front of the car and support it properly and remove the right front wheel.

4. Remove the vacuum tank retaining nuts and remove the tank from the right fender apron and set it to one side.

5. Remove the 15 fender apron retaining bolts and the fender to apron brace.

6. Move the fender apron inboard and lower it for access to the blower motor.

7. Remove the four blower motor mounting plate screws and disconnect the motor vent hose.

8. Pry the hood hinge support upward for clearance and remove the blower motor and wheel assembly.

1973–77

1. Disconnect the blower motor wires and pull the wires out of the clip at the resistor, Fig. 69.

2. Raise the front of the car and support it properly and remove the

right front wheel.

3. Locate the access opening area as shown in Fig. 70, and clean this area of the fender apron.

4. Drill a one inch hole tangent to the centerline of the bead using the dimple provided in the apron ½″ from the centerline of the bead. Take care to avoid damaging the heater case with the drill as it goes through the panel.

5. Cut out the access opening along the centerline of the bead using snips. Do not use a sabre saw or you may damage the heater case. Smooth any rough metal edges.

6. Remove the four blower motor mounting plate screws and disconnect the cooler tube from the motor.

7. Carefully move the motor and wheel assembly forward out of the heater case and through the access hole.

8. When replacing the motor and wheel assembly, obtain a cover plate to be installed over the hole.

Models With Air Conditioning

The procedure for models with air conditioning is the same as those previously given for models without air conditioning.

HEATER CORE REMOVAL

The heater core may have to be removed because it is leaking or clogged and thus producing very little heat. You can remove the heater core yourself and take it to the local radiator repair shop to have it attended to.

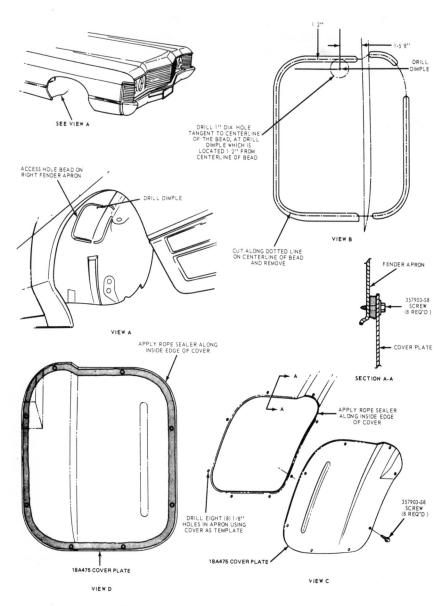

Fig. 70   *Blower access hole in fender*

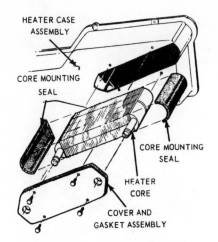

Fig. 71   Heater core details (without air conditioning)

Here is how to proceed to remove the heater core.

Models Without Air Conditioning

1. Drain the cooling system into a suitable pan.
2. Disconnect the heater hoses from the tubes at the engine side of the dash.
3. Remove the core cover and gasket and remove the heater core, Fig. 71.

Models With Air Conditioning

1. Drain the cooling system into a suitable pan.
2. Remove the carburetor air cleaner assembly.
3. Remove the two screws attaching the vacuum manifold to the dash above the heater core. Disconnect the vacuum hoses as necessary and position the manifold away from the heater core cover.

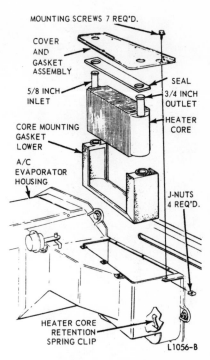

Fig. 72   Heater core details (with air conditioning)

4. Disconnect the heater hoses from the heater core tubes.
5. Remove the seven heater core cover attaching screws and remove the core cover and gasket, Fig. 72.
6. Remove the heater core from the housing.

INSTRUMENT CLUSTER REMOVAL

In order to service the speedometer or other instruments, it is first necessary for you to remove the cluster assembly. After removal of the cluster,

87

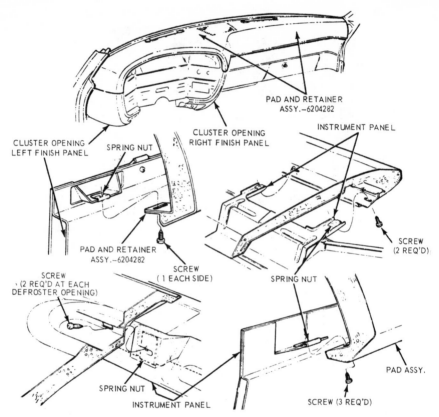

PAD AND RETAINER
ASSY.—6204282

INSTRUMENT PANEL

CLUSTER OPENING
RIGHT FINISH PANEL

CLUSTER OPENING
LEFT FINISH PANEL

SPRING NUT

SCREW
(2 REQ'D)

PAD AND RETAINER
ASSY.—6204282

SCREW
(1 EACH SIDE)

SCREW
(2 REQ'D AT EACH
DEFROSTER OPENING)

SPRING NUT

PAD ASSY.

SPRING NUT

INSTRUMENT PANEL

SCREW (3 REQ'D)

Fig. 73   Instrument panel pad removal. 1970

it is a simple matter to get at the inoperative unit.

Here's how to proceed.

1970

1. You must first remove the instrument panel pad. Refer to Fig. 73, and remove all eleven of the retaining screws, disconnect the radio speaker and remove the pad from the panel. Disconnect the battery ground cable before starting.

2. From behind the cluster, disconnect the plugs to the printed circuit, radio, Heater and A/C fan, windshield wiper and any other electrical lead to the cluster.

3. Disconnect the heater and A/C control cables and the speedometer cable.

4. Remove the power antenna rear support (1 bolt), if so equipped.

5. Remove the lighter element and all control knobs and then remove the ten cluster trim cover attaching screws, Fig. 74.

6. Remove the eight mounting screws and withdraw the cluster from the panel.

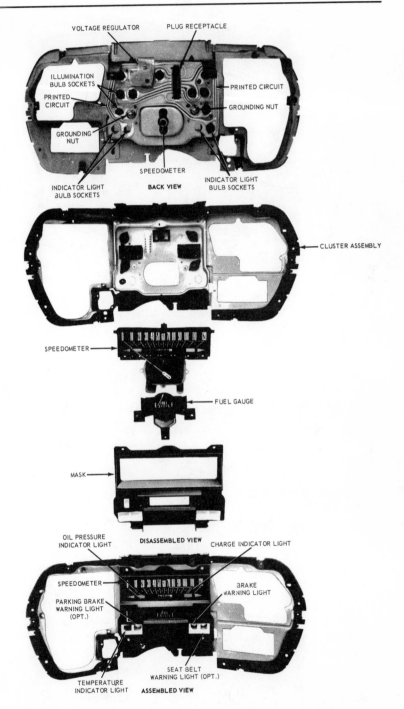

Fig. 74 Instrument cluster. 1970

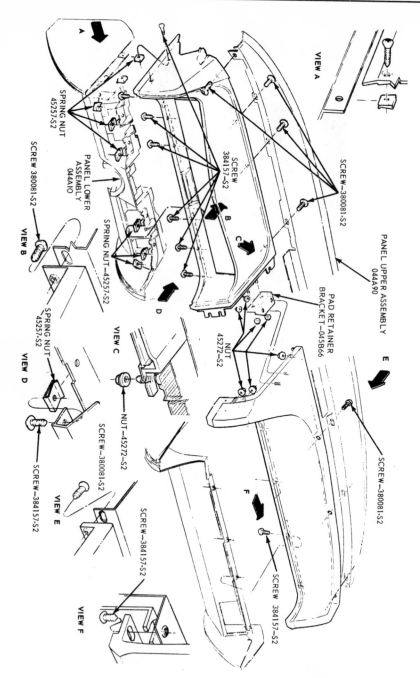

Fig. 75   Instrument panel pad removal. 1971-72

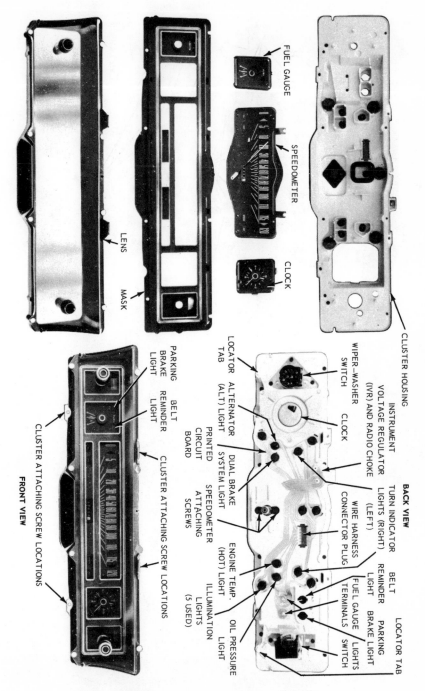

Fig. 76   Instrument cluster. 1971-72

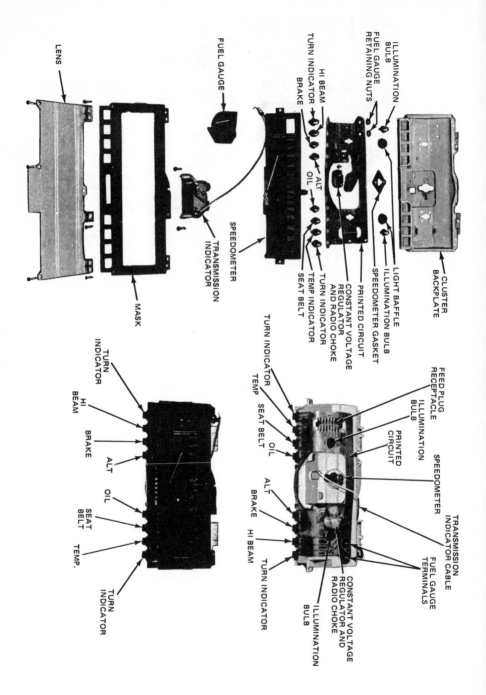

Fig. 77   Instrument cluster. 1973-77

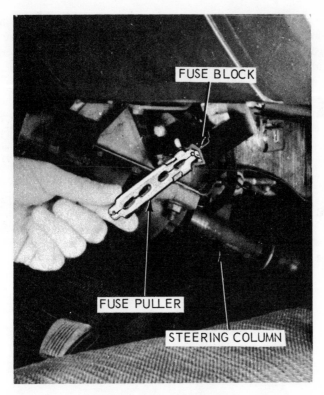

Fig. 78   Removing fuse

1971–72

1. It is first necessary to remove the instrument panel trim cover. Remove the fourteen screws, Fig. 75, retaining the pad to the panel. Disconnect the radio speaker and remove the instrument panel pad and the upper finish panel assembly. Remove five nuts and eight screws and then remove the pad and retainer from the cluster opening finish panel assembly and the upper instrument finish panel. Disconnect battery ground cable before starting.

2. Disconnect speedometer cable and the wire plugs to the rear of the cluster.

3. Remove the four cluster attaching screws and lift the cluster from the panel, Fig. 76.

1973–77

1. Disconnect the battery ground cable.

2. Remove the two lower steering column cover attaching screws and remove the lower cover.

3. Remove the two instrument cluster trim cover attaching screws and remove the trim cover.

4. Reach behind the cluster and dis-

connect the cluster feed plug.

5. Disconnect the speedometer cable and unsnap and remove the steering column shroud cover.

6. Remove the screw attaching the transmission indicator cable to the column.

7. Remove the four cluster attaching screws and remove the cluster assembly, Fig. 77.

FUSE REPLACEMENT

Should an electrical circuit cease to function it is a good bet that a fuse has blown. The fuse panel is located behind the dash to the left of the steering column. Remove the fuse in question and examine it to see if the thin wire inside the glass tube is broken. Sometimes the glass will appear blackened which would indicate the fuse has blown. A clamp type clothespin, which resembles the tool shown in Fig. 78, can easily be modified to help in pulling fuses from the fuse block.

If you are in doubt as to whether or not the fuse is blown, try another one of the same size and amperage. Check the fuse chart following and remove a good fuse from your panel and try it in place of the suspected one. It is a good idea to carry extra fuses of the size that protects your outside lights and windshield wiper.

FUSE DATA

The following list tells you the fuse size, its location and the circuit it protects

Circuit	Location	Amps
1970		
Seat Belt Warning Indicator		
Parking Brake Indicator		
Rear Defroster		
Door Ajar Indicator		
Low Fuel Light	Fuse Block	20
Power Window Relay		
Speed Control		
Emergency Warning & Cigar Lighter		
Back-up Lights & Radio Unit		
Courtesy & Dome Lights		
Map, Glove Box & Trunk Lights		
C Piller & Cargo Light		
Automatic Seat Release	Fuse Block	14
Heater & Defroster		
Throttle Solenoid		
Instrument Panel Courtesy Lights		
Radio, Ash Tray & Clock Lights		
Instrument Panel Lights		
Fuel Gauge	Fuse Block	4
Shift Quadrant Light		
Heater & A/C Controls		
Air Cond. Dealer Installed	In Line	20

Circuit	Location	Amps

1971

Emergency Warning & Cigar Lighter ....
Seat Belt Warning Indicator ....
Parking Brake, Release Warning ....
Rear Defroster ....
Power Window Relay .... } Fuse Block 20
Cornering Lamp ....
Back-up & Radio Feed ....
W/S Washer ....

Heater & Defroster ....
Warning Lamps ....
Emission & Carb. Solenoid ....
Courtesy & Dome Lamps ....
Instrument Panel & Glove Box .... } Fuse Block 14
"C" Pillar & Cargo Lamp ....
Map & Luggage Compt. Lamps ....
Clock & Ignition Key Buzzer ....
Auto. Seat Back Latch ....

Instrument Panel Illum. ....
Clock Radio & Heater Switch ....
A/C Controls & Ash Tray ....
Shift Indicator & Speed .... } Fuse Block 4
Ammeter & Fuel Gauge ....
Turn Signal Indicator Lights ....
High Beam Indicator ....
Air Cond. (Dealer Install.) .... In Line 20

1972

Emergency Warning ....
Cigar Lighter ....
Back-Up Lamps ....
Radio Feed ....} Fuse Block 20
Accessory Feed ....
W/S Washer ....
Speed Control Relay ....

Warning Lamps ....
Heater & Defroster ....
Courtesy & Dome Lamps ....
Instrument Panel & Glove Box .... } Fuse Block 14
"C" Pillar & Cargo Lamps ....
Map & Cargo Comp. Lamps ....

Clock & Ignition Key Buzzer ....
Indicator Lamp ....
Parking Brake ....} Fuse Block 75
Radio, Stereo Tape Player ....

Instruments ....
Speedometer & Fuel Gauge ....
Shift Indicator ....} Fuse Block 4
Heater ....
A/C, Clock, Radio & Ash Tray ....

1973-74

Rear Window Defroster ....
Cornering Lamps ....
Speed Control Relay ....} Fuse Block 20
W/S Washer (1973) ....

	Circuit	Location	Amps
Cigar Lighter			
Hazard Warning & Stop Lamps			
Courtesy & Back-Up Lamps			
Instrument Panel			
Dome & Glove Box Lamps		Fuse Block	15
Luggage Compartment			
Clock & Ignition Key Buzzer			
Heater & A/C			
W/S Washer			
Indicator Lamp			
Parking Brake		Fuse Block	7.5
Radio, Stereo Tape Player			
Cluster Illum.			
A/C & ATC Control			
clock, Radio & Ash Tray		Fuse Block	4
Headlamp & W/S Switch			

1975-76

Circuit	Location	Amps
A/C Blower Motor	Fuse Block	30
Tailgate Window	Fuse Block	25
Power Windows (2 Dr. Models)	Fuse Block	20 C.B.
W/S Washer & Speed Control		
Rear Window Deice Relay & Trunk Release		
Power Window Safety Relay (4 Dr. Models)	Fuse Block	20
Cornering Lamps		
Heater Blower Motor & A/C Clutch		
Turn Signal & Back-up Lamps		
Radio, Tape Player & Power Antenna		
Dome, Courtesy & Glove Box Lamps		
Trunk Lamp & Anti-Theft Module	Fuse Block	15
Key Buzzer & Seatback Latch Relay		
Clock & Lighter		
Stop & Hazard Warning Lamps	Fuse Block	15
W/S Wiper	Fuse Block	8.25 C.B.
Tell Tale Lamps & Throttle Solenoid	Fuse Block	7.5
Instrument Panel Lamps	Fuse Block	4
Headlamps	Light Switch	18 C.B.
Parking, Tail & License Lamps		
Side Marker Lamps & Horn	Light Switch	15 C.B.
Power Windows (4 Dr. Models)		
Power Seat & Seat Back Latch	Starter Relay	20 C.B.
Power Door Locks & Underhood Lamp		
Speed Control	In Line	30
Rear Window Deice	In Line	30

1977

Circuit	Location	Amps
AM, AM/FM Radio, Stereotape	Fuse Block	15
Warning Lights	Fuse Block	7.5
Windshield Washer, Rear Window Defugger		
Power Window Relay, Cornering Lights	Fuse Block	20
Speed Control, Rear Door Cigar Lighters		
Trunk Release		

Circuit	Location	Amps
Windshield Wiper	Fuse Block	8.25 C.B.
Station Wagon Rear Window		
Power Windows (2 Dr. Models)	} Fuse Block 25	
Instrument Cluster, Clock		
Radio, Ashtray, Headlight Switch		
W/S Wiper Switch, Heater	} Fuse Block 4	
A/C control		
Heater, A/C	Fuse Block 30	
Back Up Lights		
Turn Signals	} Fuse Block 20	
A/C Clutch		
Courtesy Lights, Domelight		
Glove Box, Trunk or Cargo		
Clock Feed, Key Warning Buzzer	} Fuse Block 15	
Seatback Latch		
Hazard Flasher System		
Stop Lights	} Fuse Block 15	
Cigar Lighter	Fuse Block 15	
Headlamps	Light Switch . 18 C.B.	
Power Windows	Fuse Block .. 20 C.B.	
Rear Window Defogger	In Line 30	
Parking, Tail & License	Light Switch . 15 C.B.	

LAMP BULB DATA

The following list provides the various bulb numbers
and their functions.

Location	Bulb No.
1970-71	
Back-Up Lights	1156
Clock Light	194
Courtesy Lights—	
1970	105
1971	562
Dome Light	105
Glove Box Lights—	
1970	1816
1971	1893
Headlamp (Type 1)	4001
Headlamp (Type 2)	4002
High Beam Indicator	194
Instrument Panel	194
License Plate Light	97
Parking Brake Indicator	194
Parking Light & Turn Signal—	
1970	1157
1971	1157NA

Location	Bulb No.
Radio Dial Light—	
1970	194
1971	1893
Shift Dial Indicator	1445
Side Marker Lights	194
Stop, Tail & Turn Signal	1157
Tell-Tale Indicator	194
Trunk Light	631
Turn Signal Indicator	194
1972-74	
Back-Up Lights	1156
Clock Lights	194
Cornering Light—	
1972	1196
1973-74	1295
Courtesy Lights	631
Dome Light	561

Location	Bulb No.	Location	Bulb No.

Glove Box Light—
1972 1816
1973 158
1974 194
Headlamp (Type 1) 4001
Headlamp (Type 2)—
1972 4002
1973-74 4000
High Beam Indicator Light 194
Instrument Panel Lights 194
License Plate Light—
1972 97
1973 94
1974 Exc. Sta. Wag. 1178
1974 Sta. Wag. 90
Parking Brake Indicator Light 194
Parking Lights—
1972 .... 1157NA
1973 1157
1974 Front 97A
1974 Rear 194
Radio Dial Light 1893
Seat Belt Indicator 194
Shift Dial Light 1891
Side Marker Lights—
Exc. Below 194
1973 Front 97NA
1973 Rear 94
Stop & Tail Lights 1157
Tell Tale Lights 194
Trunk Light 631
Turn Signal Lights—
Exc. Below 1157
1972 Front 1157NA
Turn Signal Indicator Light 194

1975-76

Back-Up Light 1156
Brake Indicator 194
Clock Light 194
Cornering Light 1295
Courtesy Light—   C-Pillar 105
Door 214-2
Instrument Panel—
1975 631
1976 89
Dome Light—
Exc. Below 211-2
1976 Less Map Lamp 561
Glove Compartment Light 194
Headlamp (Type 1) 4001
Headlamp (Type 2) 4000
High Beam Indicator 194
Instrument Light 194
License Plate Light—
Exc. Station Wagon 1178
Station Wagon 194

Parking Light 1157NA
Radio Dial Light—
Exc. Below 1893
1975 AM-FM Stereo Radio 37
1976 AM-FM Stereo Radio With Tape
Player 37
Seat Belt Indicator 194
Side Marker Light—
Sedan—
Front (Mercury) 97NA
Rear (Mercury) 168
Station Wagon Rear 194
Stop Light & Tail Light 1157
Tell-Tale Lights 194
Trunk Light—
1975 631
1976 89
Turn Signal—
Front 1157NA
Rear 1157
Turn Signal Indicator 194

1977

Headlights - Hi & Lo 4000
Headlights - High Beam 4001
**Front Park & Turn Signal (Hi and
Lo)** 1157NA
Taillights/Stop/Turn Signal - Sedan   1157
Taillights/Stop/Turn Signal - Sta
Wgn. 1157
Back-Up Lights 1156
License Plate Light - Sta Wgn 194
License Plate Light - Sedan 168
Dome Light 561
Instrument Courtesy Light 89
Cargo Lights - Sta Wgn 105
Rear Side Marker (Sta Wgn.) 194
High Beam Indicators 194
Turn Signal Indicators 194
**Warning Lights - Alt-Brake-Seat
Belt-Engine** 194
Instrument Illumination Light 194
Heater Control Panel 161
Headlight—Wiper-Wash Illumination . 161
Dome Light 211-2
Map Light 105
Glove Box Light 194
Cornering Lights-Hi Series 1295
Luggage Compartment 89
Ash Tray Light 161
Clock 194
**Rear Window Electric Defog
Light** .... D3AB-18C622-A A
Engine Compartment Light 89
Parking Brake Light 194

Location	Bulb No.	Location	Bulb No.
Visor Vanity	212-2	AM/FM Stereo Tape (2 req'd)	37
Radio Pilot Light		AM/FM Quadrasonic Tape	37
AM	1893	AM/FM Stereo Search	37
AM/FM Monaural	1893	Radio Stereo Light	
AM/FM Stereo	1893	AM/FM Stereo	1892

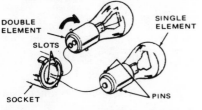

DOUBLE ELEMENT   SINGLE ELEMENT   SLOTS   SOCKET   PINS

DEPRESS BULB IN SOCKET AND ROTATE COUNTERCLOCKWISE. THEN, PULL BULB FROM SOCKET.

TO INSTALL, INSPECT PINS ON BULB BASE. IF THEY ARE NOT SAME DISTANCE FROM BOTTOM OF BASE, THEY MUST BE INSERTED INTO THE CORRECT SLOT. DETERMINE WHICH SLOT IN SOCKET PINS SHOULD BE INSERTED INTO AND PUSH BULB BASE INTO SOCKET. THEN, ROTATE CLOCKWISE TO ENGAGE PINS. IF BULB WILL NOT ROTATE, PINS ARE IN WRONG SLOTS.

BULB   CLIPS

INSERT A FUSE PULLER UNDER BULB AND PRY BULB OUT OF CLIPS.
TO INSTALL POSITION BULB TO CLIPS AND PRESS INTO PLACE.

SOCKET   BULB

PULL BULB STRAIGHT OUT OF SOCKET TO REMOVE.

TO INSTALL, POSITION BULB TO SOCKET AND PUSH STRAIGHT IN UNTIL SEATED.

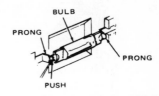

BULB   PRONG   PRONG   PUSH

TO REMOVE, PUSH PRONG TOWARD BULB AND LIFT BULB FROM PRONG.

TO INSTALL, ENGAGE ONE END OF BULB OVER ONE PRONG. THEN, PUSH OTHER PRONG TOWARD BULB AND ENGAGE BULB END OVER PRONG. DO NOT FORCE BULB END OVER PRONG.

Fig. 79   Various lamp bulbs

Cooling System

Earlier in this book, we provided the help necessary in caring for the hoses, belts, thermostat and the coolant in the system. In this section, we will help you to remove the radiator, which may be leaking or blocked, so you can take it to the radiator repair shop for the necessary repair. We will also help you to remove the water pump, in the event yours has failed or is leaky or noisy.

RADIATOR REMOVAL

If your car radiator is leaking or blocked causing engine overheating, you can save a big part of the repair cost by removing the radiator yourself and taking it to the radiator repair shop.

Here's how you can remove the radiator:

1. Drain the cooling system into a

suitable pan.

2. Disconnect the upper and lower hoses from the raditor.

3. If car has an automatic transmission, disconnect the transmission fluid cooler lines from the radiator.

4. If equipped with fan shroud, remove the upper bolts attaching the shroud to the radiator support and lift the shroud enough to disengage it and lay it back over the fan.

5. Remove the radiator upper support attaching bolts and remove the support.

6. Carefully lift the radiator from the car.

WATER PUMP REPLACEMENT

New and rebuilt water pumps are available at your local auto parts supply store. This is a good time for you to also check the hoses, belts and the condition of the coolant. If your water pump is leaking, you may well have lost a good portion of the coolant. Plan to drain and flush the system and refill it with fresh coolant in at least a 50% solution with water.

Here's the procedure to follow in replacing the water pump:

Six Cylinder

1. Drain the cooling system into a suitable pan.

2. Loosen and remove the alternator, power steering and air conditioning drive belts.

3. Disconnect the radiator lower hose and the heater hose at the water pump.

4. Remove the fan, spacer, pulley and drive belt.

5. Remove the four bolts attaching the pump to the engine and remove the pump.

V8–302, 351W

1. Drain the cooling system into a suitable pan.

2. On cars equipped with a fan shroud, remove the shroud attaching bolts and position the shroud over the fan.

3. Remove the fan and spacer from the pump shaft and remove the shroud, if used.

4. If car is air conditioned, remove the drive belt and idler pulley bracket.

5. Remove the alternator belt and if equipped with power steering, remove the belt and the power steering pump.

6. Remove all brackets attached to the water pump and the water pump pulley.

7. Disconnect hoses at water pump and unfasten and remove pump.

V8–351C, 351M, 400

1. Drain the cooling system into a suitable pan.

2. Disconnect the battery ground cable to prevent accidental shorts.

3. Remove the fan shroud attaching bolts and position the shroud over the fan.

4. If the car is air conditioned, remove the compressor drive belt lower idler pulley and the compressor mount to water pump bracket.
5. Loosen the alternator and remove the drive belt.
6. If car has power steering, loosen the power steering pump and remove the drive belt.
7. Remove the water pump pulley.
8. Remove any brackets attached to the water pump and position out of way.
9. Disconnect the heater hose from the water pump.
10. Remove the water pump attaching bolts and remove the pump.

V8–390

1. Drain the cooling system into a suitable pan.
2. Remove the bolts and nuts attaching the power steering pump mounting bracket. Remove the pump and bracket assembly to one side.
3. Remove power steering, air conditioning and air pump drive belts.
4. Disconnect the radiator lower hose and heater hose at the water pump.
5. Remove the radiator upper support and fan guard.
6. Remove the fan, fan spacer or fan drive clutch and pulley.
7. Remove the four bolts attaching the pump to the engine and remove the pump.

V8-429, 460

1. Drain the cooling system into a suitable pan and remove the fan shroud attaching bolts.
2. Remove bolts attaching fan to water pump and remove fan and shroud.
3. If car has power steering, loosen power steering pump attaching bolts.
4. If car has air conditioning, loosen compressor attaching bolts and remove the air conditioning and power steering drive belts.
5. Loosen the alternator pivot bolt and remove the two attaching bolts and spacer. Remove the belt and rotate the bracket out of the way.
6. If car has Thermactor air pump, remove the pump pulley and the pump pivot bolt. Remove the air pump adjusting bracket at the pump and remove the upper bracket attaching bolt and swing the bracket out of the way.
7. Remove air conditioning compressor attaching bolts and secure compressor to the left fender brace.
8. Remove power steering pump bolts and position pump to one side.
9. Remove air conditioning bracket attaching bolts and remove bracket.
10. Disconnect hoses from water pump and unfasten and remove pump.

Brakes

Before performing any brake work on your car, examine the back side of the wheels to see if there is any evidence of hydraulic fluid leakage. If the back sides of the wheels are wet from hydraulic fluid leakage, it is suggested the car be taken to a professional mechanic who is skilled in these repairs. If no leakage is evident, then you can proceed with the brake shoe replacement. When replacing brake shoes or disc pads, disassemble one side at a time so that you can refer to the other side for proper installation of parts.

If your brake drums or discs are found to be deeply scored, they should be taken to an automotive machine shop to be refinished before installation.

FRONT WHEEL DISC BRAKE PAD REPLACEMENT

If you have noticed that your brake pedal must be pushed closer to the floor than usual, or if you have been hearing a scraping, screeching noise coming from the front when you apply the brakes, the chances are the pads are worn and the rivets are scraping against the brake disc. Continued use in this condition will only lead to a more expensive brake job requiring the brake discs to be machined. You should also check the master cylinder, under the hood, to see if the brake fluid level is low. If there are no hydraulic system leaks, this would be a confirming sign of worn brake pads.

Plan to check the brake system immediately if any of these conditions are present.

1970–72

1. Raise the front of the car and support it properly on stands.
2. Remove the wheel and tire assembly. Be careful to avoid damage or interference with the caliper splash shield or bleeder screw fitting.
3. Disconnect the brake hose from the caliper and cap the hose to prevent loss of brake fluid.
4. Remove the caliper locating pins, Figs. 80, 81 and 82, and lower stabilizer attaching bolts and discard the stabilizer.
5. Lift the caliper from the anchor plate.
6. Remove the inner brake shoe hold down clips from the anchor plate, remove the locating pin insulators from the anchor plate and remove the inboard brake pad.
7. To remove the outer pad, place a small screwdriver under the outer brake shoe retaining clip tang and lift away from the pin groove and slide the clip from the brake shoe retaining pin. Remove the other brake shoe retaining clip and remove the outer pad.
8. When installing new brake pads, it will be necessary to first retract the piston in the caliper to make room for the new thicker pads. An old brake pad can be used to fabricate a tool for retracting the piston, Figs. 83 and 84.

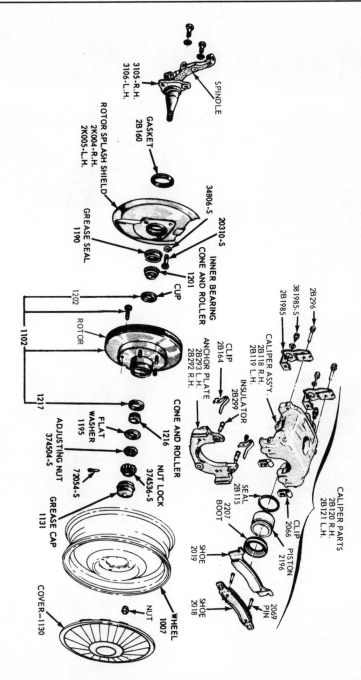

Fig. 80   Disc brake exploded. 1970-72

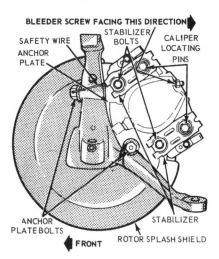

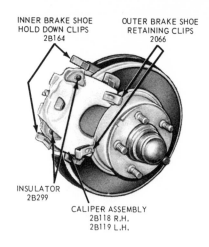

Fig. 82   Caliper details. 1970-72

Fig. 81   Removing caliper locating pins. 1970-72

1973–77

1. Raise the front of the car and support it properly on stands.
2. Remove the tire and wheel assembly.

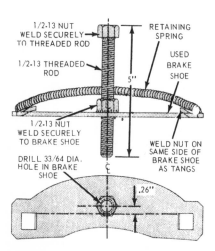

Fig. 83   Fabricating tool. 1970-72

3. Remove the retaining screw from the caliper retaining key, Fig. 85 and 86.
4. Slide the retaining key and support spring either inward or outward from the anchor plate. Use a hammer and drift, if necessary, but be careful to avoid damaging the key.
5. Lift the caliper assembly away from the anchor plate by pushing the caliper downward against the plate, and rotating the upper end upward and out of the anchor plate. Use care so that the flexible brake hose is not stretched or twisted.
6. Remove the inner pad and lining from the anchor plate. If the pad anti-rattle clip (inner pad only) becomes displaced, reposition it on the anchor plate, Fig. 87. Tap lightly on the outer pad and lining to free it from the caliper.
7. When installing new pads, use a 4 inch C-clamp and a block of wood 1¾″ x 1″ and about ¾″ thick to

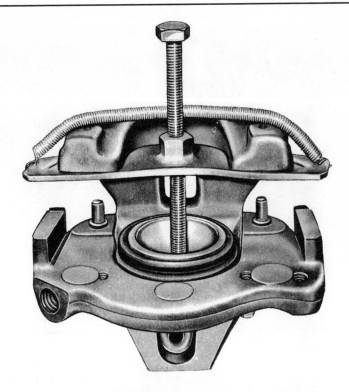

Fig. 84   Installing piston retracting tool. 1970-72

force the caliper piston back into its bore to make room for the thicker new pads.

REAR WHEEL DISC BRAKE PAD REPLACEMENT

1976–77

1. Raise the rear of the car and support it properly on stands.
2. Remove the wheel and tire assemblies from the axle.
3. Disconnect the parking brake cable from the lever, Fig. 88. Be careful not to kink or cut the cable or return spring.
4. Remove the retaining screw from

the caliper retaining key, Fig. 89.
5. Slide the caliper retaining key and support spring from the anchor plate. Use a hammer and a soft drift and use care to avoid damaging the key or sliding ways or hitting the parking brake lever.
6. Lift the caliper assembly away from the anchor plate by pushing the caliper downward against the anchor plate and then rotating the upper end out of the anchor plate. If rust build-up on the outer edge of the rotor braking surface prevents removal, scrape the loose scale from the edges with a putty knife being careful not to gouge or mar the braking surfaces. When

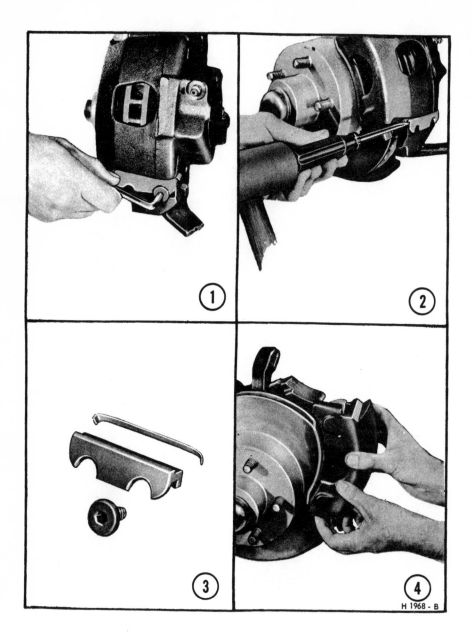

Fig. 85   Removing caliper. 1973-77

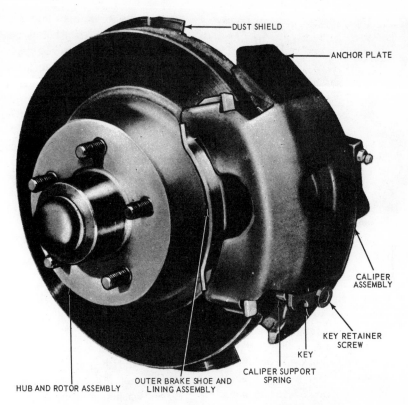

Fig. 86   Disc brake details. 1973-77

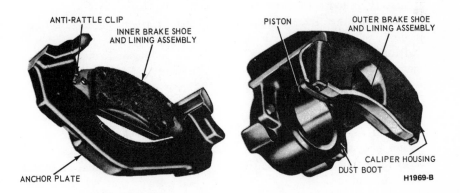

Fig. 87   Outer shoe removal. 1973-77

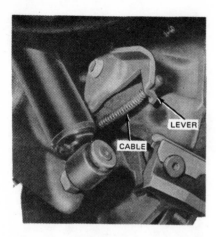

Fig. 88   Parking brake lever and cable

rotor wear or scoring prevents caliper removal, it is necessary to loosen the caliper end retainer ½ turn maximum, to allow the piston to be forced back into its bore. To loosen the end retainer, remove the parking brake lever, then mark or scribe the end retainer and caliper housing to be sure the end retainer is not loosened more than ½ turn. Force the piston back into its bore and move the caliper back and forth to center the rotor and then remove the caliper.

7. Remove the inner shoe and lining from the anchor plate. The brake shoe antirattle clip may be displaced. If so, reposition it to the anchor plate. Tap lightly on the outer shoe and lining to free it from the caliper.

FRONT DRUM BRAKE SHOES REPLACEMENT

When you have to push the brake

pedal closer to the floor than usual to stop the car, or when noises coming from the wheels when you apply the brakes cause all heads to turn, we advise you to remove one of the wheel and hub assemblies and inspect the brake shoes. If the linings are worn to within $1/32''$ of the rivet heads, they should be replaced. Continued operation in this condition will lead to serious scoring of the brake drums which will necessitate their having to be machined to remove the grooves cut into them by the rivet heads.

Proceed as follows, to replace the brake shoes:

1. Raise the car and support it properly on stands.
2. Remove the hub cap or disc from the wheel.
3. Remove the grease cap from the hub and then remove the cotter pin, nut lock, adjusting nut and flat washer from the spindle. Remove the outer bearing cone and roller assembly.
4. Pull the drum off the spindle. If the drum will not come off, pry the rubber cover from the back side of the brake backing plate. Insert a narrow screwdriver through the slot and disengage the adjusting lever from the adjusting screw. While holding the adjusting lever away from the screw, back off the adjusting screw with a brake adjusting tool or another screwdriver, Fig. 92. Be careful not to burr, chip or damage the notches in the adjusting screw; otherwise the self-adjusting mechanism will not operate properly.

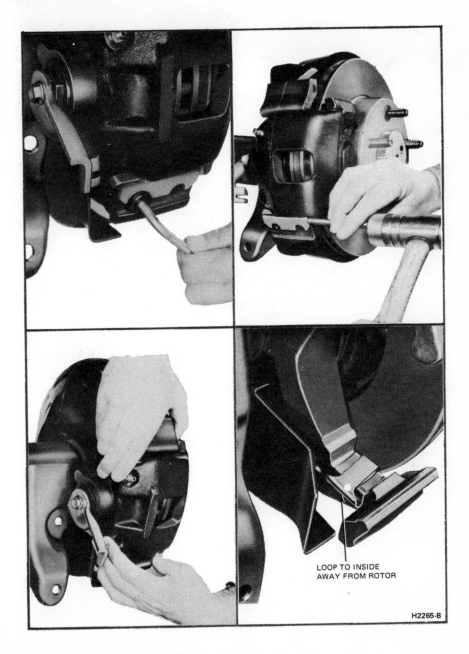

LOOP TO INSIDE
AWAY FROM ROTOR

H2265-B

Fig. 89   Removing rear caliper

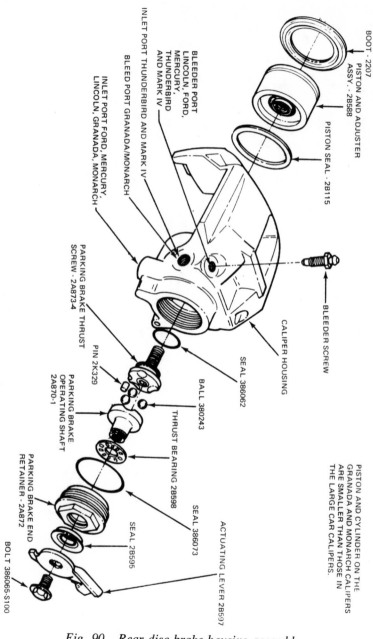

BOOT - 2207

PISTON AND ADJUSTER
ASSY. - 2B588

PISTON SEAL - 2B115

BLEEDER PORT
LINCOLN, FORD,
MERCURY,
THUNDERBIRD
AND MARK IV

INLET PORT THUNDERBIRD AND MARK IV

BLEED PORT GRANADA/MONARCH

INLET PORT FORD, MERCURY,
LINCOLN, GRANADA, MONARCH

PARKING BRAKE THRUST
SCREW - 2A873-4

PIN 2K329

PARKING BRAKE
OPERATING SHAFT
2A870-1

PARKING BRAKE END
RETAINER - 2A872

BOLT 386065-S100

SEAL 2B595

SEAL 386073

THRUST BEARING 2B598

BALL 380243

SEAL 386062

ACTUATING LEVER 2B597

CALIPER HOUSING

BLEEDER SCREW

PISTON AND CYLINDER ON THE
GRANADA AND MONARCH CALIPERS
ARE SMALLER THAN THOSE IN
THE LARGE CAR CALIPERS.

Fig. 90   Rear disc brake housing assembly

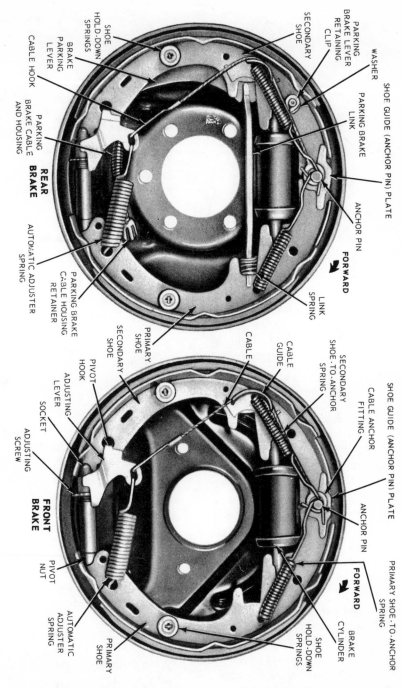

Fig. 91   Drum brake assembly details

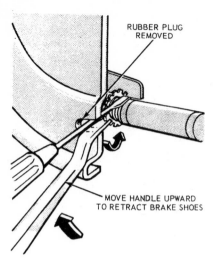

RUBBER PLUG
REMOVED

MOVE HANDLE UPWARD
TO RETRACT BRAKE SHOES

Fig. 92   Back off brake adjustment

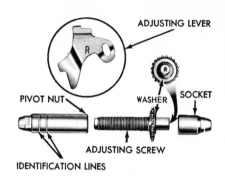

ADJUSTING LEVER

PIVOT NUT   WASHER   SOCKET

IDENTIFICATION LINES

ADJUSTING SCREW

Fig. 93   Self adjuster screw details

5. Refer to Fig. 91 for an assembled view of the brakes and remove the shoe-to-anchor springs. Unhook the cable eye from the anchor pin.
6. Remove the shoe guide (anchor pin) plate, if so equipped.
7. Remove the shoe hold down springs, shoes, adjusting screw, pivot nut, socket and automatic adjuster parts.
8. Be sure the automatic adjuster mechanism is thoroughly clean so it will operate freely. Notice that the adjusters are stamped R or L meanining Right or Left side. They must be correctly installed or the brake shoes will retract rather than adjust properly, Fig. 93.
9. Clean the brake backing plate and apply a light coating of brakelube to the pad surfaces where the shoes contact the backing plate.
10. After installation of parts, check operation of adjuster by pulling on cable far enough to lift the adjust-

ing lever past a tooth on the adjusting screw. When the cable is released the lever should snap into position behind the next tooth. This action adjusts the shoes.
11. Using a brake shoe/drum adjusting tool, fit the tool into the drum until snug and tighten the nut, Fig. 94. Now remove the tool and fit it over the assembled brake shoes. Rotate the tool over the shoes to be sure of the setting, Fig. 95. If the tool will not fit over the shoes, hold the adjusting lever out of engagement while rotating the adjusting screw to retract the shoes until the tool fits properly over them.
12. Final adjustment can be made after assembly is completed and the car is lowered by making a few reverse and forward stops. This action on a reverse stop following a forward stop, allows the adjuster to expand the shoes until all excessive clearance between shoes and drum is eliminated.

REAR DRUM BRAKE SHOES REPLACEMENT

1. Raise the rear of the car and sup-

port it properly on stands.

2. Remove the tire and wheel assembly.

3. Remove the drum retainer nuts from the axle studs and remove the drum. If the drum will not come off, pry the rubber cover from the back side of the brake backing plate. Insert a narrow screwdriver through the hole and disengage the adjusting lever from the adjusting screw. Then use a brake adjusting tool or another screwdriver to back off the adjuster to permit drum removal. Be careful to avoid damaging the teeth on the adjusting screw or the self adjusting mechanism will not operate properly.

4. Remove the shoe-to-anchor springs and unhook the cable eye from the anchor pin.

5. Remove the shoe guide (anchor pin) plate, if so equipped.

6. Remove the shoe hold down springs, shoes, adjusting screw, pivot nut, socket and automatic adjuster parts.

7. Remove the parking brake link, spring and retainer. Disconnect the parking brake cable from the parking brake lever.

8. After removing the rear brake secondary shoe, disassemble the parking brake lever from the shoe by removing the retaining clip and spring washer.

9. Be sure the automatic adjuster mechanism is thoroughly clean so it will operate freely. Notice that the adjusters are stamped R or L meaning Right or Left side. They must be properly installed or the brake shoes will retract rather than

adjust the shoes properly.

10. Clean the brake backing plate and apply a light coating of brakelube to the pad surfaces where the shoes contact the backing plate.

11. After reassembly of parts, check operation of adjuster by pulling on the cable far enough to lift the adjusting lever past a tooth on the adjusting screw. When the cable is released the lever should snap into position behind the next tooth. This action adjusts the shoes.

12. Using a brake shoe/drum adjusting tool, fit the tool into the drum until snug and tighten the nut, Fig. 94. Now remove the tool and fit it over the assembled brake shoes. Rotate the tool over the shoes to be sure of the setting, Fig. 95. If the tool will not fit over the shoes, hold the adjusting lever out of engagement while rotating the adjusting screw to retract the shoes until the tool fits properly over them.

13. Final adjustment can be made after assembly is completed and the car is lowered by making a few reverse and forward stops. This action on a reverse stop followed by a forward stop, allows the adjuster to expand the shoes until all excessive clearance between shoes and drum is eliminated.

FRONT WHEEL BEARING ADJUSTMENT

After brake service or when looseness exists, the front wheel bearings

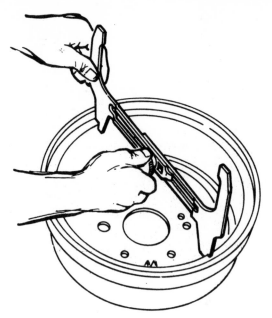

Fig. 94   Measuring brake drum inside diameter

should be checked for proper adjustment.

1. Block the rear wheels and raise the front of the car and support it properly on stands.
2. Pry off the hub cap or wheel cover and remove the grease cap from the wheel hub, Fig. 96.
3. Wipe off the excess grease from the end of the spindle and remove the cotter pin and the nut lock.
4. If the car is equipped with disc brakes, loosen the bearing adjusting nut three turns and rock the wheel in and out several times to push the brake pads away from the brake rotor.
5. On all models, while turning the wheel assembly, tighten the adjusting nut to 17–25 ft. lbs. to seat the bearings, Fig. 97.
6. Now back off the adjusting nut exactly ½ turn. Then tighten the nut to 10–15 in. lbs. or finger tight.
7. Place the nut lock on the adjusting nut so that one of the cotter pin holes will align with one of the castellations of the nut lock. Install a new cotter pin and bend its ends around the flange of the nut lock.
8. Check wheel rotation to be sure it rotates freely and install the grease cap and hub cap.
9. Lower the car and if equipped with disc brakes, pump the brake pedal several times before driving the car to establish lining to rotor clearance and restore normal pedal travel.

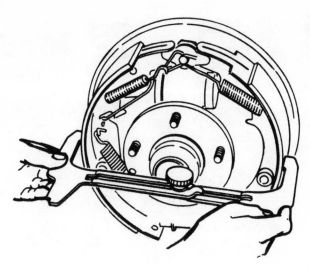

Fig. 95   Adjusting brake shoes

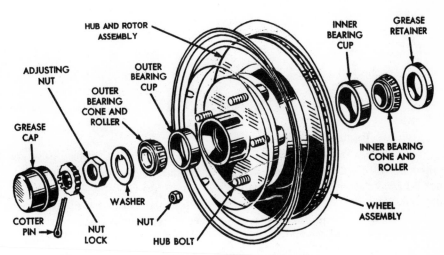

Fig. 96   Front wheel hub details

PARKING BRAKE ADJUSTMENT

If the parking brake fails to hold the car, after its having been applied, it should be adjusted as outlined immediately following. (If an adjustment does not correct the condition, check the rear brake shoes for excessive wear).

1. Make sure the parking brake is fully released.

115

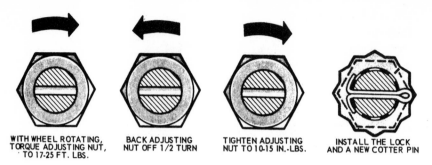

WITH WHEEL ROTATING, TORQUE ADJUSTING NUT, TO 17-25 FT. LBS.   BACK ADJUSTING NUT OFF 1/2 TURN   TIGHTEN ADJUSTING NUT TO 10-15 IN.-LBS.   INSTALL THE LOCK AND A NEW COTTER PIN

Fig. 97   Front wheel bearing adjustment

2. Raise the rear of the car and support it properly on stands placed under the rear axle.
3. Tighten the adjusting nut against the cable equalizer (beneath the car) to cause rear wheel brake drag.

4. Then, loosen the adjusting nut until the rear brakes are fully released. There should be no brake drag. Tighten the lock nut.
5. Lower the car and check operation of the parking brake.

Suspension

Properly acting shock absorbers are important to safe driving. They function to keep the tires in contact with the road and if they are worn the wheels will hop on the road surface causing a loss of steering and braking control. This condition will also lead to cupped tires from the constant wheel hopping.

You can perform a simple test on your shock absorbers. Merely push down on one of the front fenders as far down as you can push. Without letting go, pull it upward as far as you can. Continue this motion through several more cycles. Release the car at the top of the cycle. It should settle after moving to the bottom of the cycle and part way up. If the car continues to bounce, the shocks are worn and should be replaced. Perform this same test on the remaining three corners of the car.

FRONT SHOCK ABSORBER REPLACEMENT

1. Remove the nut, washer and bushing from the shock absorber upper end.
2. Raise the front of the car and sup-

port it properly on stands.

3. Remove two bolts attaching the shock absorber to the lower suspension arm and remove the shock absorber.

REAR SHOCK ABSORBER REPLACEMENT

1. Raise the rear of the car and support it properly on stands.
2. Remove the shock absorber attaching nut, washer and bushing from the upper stud at the upper side of the spring upper seat.
3. Compress the shock absorber to clear the hole in the spring seat and remove the inner bushing and washer from the upper attaching stud.
4. Remove the self-locking attaching nut and disconnect the shock absorber lower stud from the mounting bracket on the rear axle housing.

BALL JOINT REPLACEMENT

The procedures listed below are for replacing the upper and lower ball joints of 1970–71 models only. On all later models, the vehicle manufacturer recommends that the complete control arm be replaced and since these procedures are beyond the scope of this book it is suggested they be left to a skilled mechanic having the proper equipment.

Upper

1. Raise the car high enough to pro-

vide working space and place a support under the lower control arm.
2. Remove the wheel and tire assembly.
3. Drill a ⅛″ hole thrugh each upper ball joint rivet. Using a large chisel, cut off the rivets.
4. Remove the cotter pin and nut from the upper ball joint stud.
5. Position an expanding press tool between the upper and lower ball joint studs and expand the tool to place tension on the ball studs and then tap the spindle with a hammer near the upper stud to loosen the stud from the spindle. Do not loosen the stud with tool pressure alone. Remove the ball joint.
6. The replacement ball joint will use bolts and nuts to secure it to the suspension control arm.

Lower

1. Raise the vehicle high enough to provide working space, leaving the lower arm free to drop as coil spring tension is eased.
2. Drill a ⅛″ hole through each of the ball joint rivets. Then drill off the rivet head using a ⅜″ drill and drive the rivets out. Position a jack or safety stand under the lower suspension arm and lower the car about six inches to offset the coil spring tension.
3. Remove the cotter pin and nut from the lower ball stud.
4. Install an expanding press tool between the upper and lower ball joint studs and expand the tool to place the lower ball stud under tension.

5. Using a hammer, tap the spindle near the lower ball stud to free it from the spindle and remove the

ball joint.

6. The replacement ball joint will be secured by bolts and nuts.

Engine

Some of the procedures in this section are provided to help you through, what might seem to be, very difficult and time consuming jobs. Although they are not very difficult, they do take more time than most of the jobs presented elsewhere in this book. But with the help of this book, you will be able to do these jobs and seize the opportunity to save hundreds of dollars.

MOTOR MOUNT REPLACEMENT

The rubber portion of the motor mounts may become soft, cracked or even separated to the point that the engine is allowed to move further than it should in its mountings. This could cause stress on hoses or allow the fan to hit the radiator or its shroud. It may also lead to binding linkage at the accelerator. You can replace these worn out or broken motor mounts, and here is how to do it.

1970–72 Six

Front

1. Raise the car and support it properly on stands.
2. Loosen the nuts attaching the insulator assemblies to the intermediate support brackets, Fig. 98.

3. Position a transmission jack under the oil pan and raise the engine sufficiently to remove its weight from the supports.
4. Remove the insulator assembly to engine bolts and remove the insulator to intermediate support bracket nut and remove the insulator.

Rear

1. Remove the insulator assembly to crossmember attaching bolt and nut.
2. Raise the transmission with a jack to obtain clearance at the transmission extension housing.
3. Then remove the retainer and insulator assembly attaching bolts and washers and remove the insulator assembly and retainer.

V8–302, 351W
Front

1. Support the engine using a jack and a block of wood placed under the oil pan.
2. Remove the nut and through bolt attaching the insulator to the insulator support bracket, Fig. 99.
3. Raise the engine slightly with the jack.
4. Remove the engine insulator assembly to engine block attaching bolts.

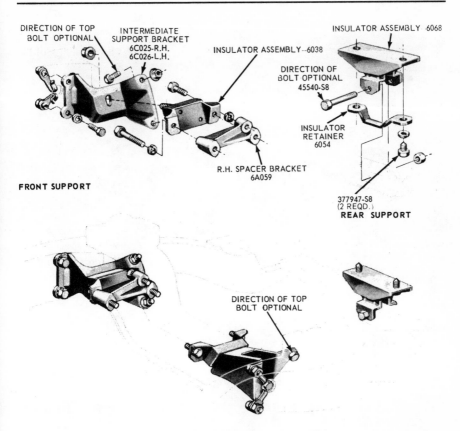

DIRECTION OF TOP
BOLT OPTIONAL

INTERMEDIATE
SUPPORT BRACKET
6C025-R.H.
6C026-L.H.

INSULATOR ASSEMBLY–6038

INSULATOR ASSEMBLY 6068

DIRECTION OF
BOLT OPTIONAL
45540-S8

INSULATOR
RETAINER
6054

R.H. SPACER BRACKET
6A059

FRONT SUPPORT

377947-S8
(2 REQD.)
REAR SUPPORT

DIRECTION OF TOP
BOLT OPTIONAL

Fig. 98   Engine supports. Six cylinder

5. Remove the engine insulator assembly and the heat shield (where used), Fig.

Rear

1. Support the engine with a jack and block of wood placed under the oil pan and remove the support insulator to crossmember through bolt and lock nut.

2. Raise the transmission with a floor jack and remove the support insulator and retainer, Fig. 100.

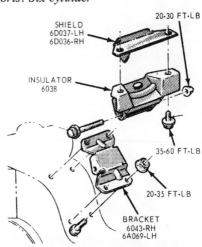

20-30 FT-LB

SHIELD
6D037-LH
6D036-RH

INSULATOR
6038

35-60 FT-LB

20-35 FT-LB

BRACKET
6043-RH
6A069-LH

*Fig. 99   Front motor mounts.
V8-302, 351W*

119

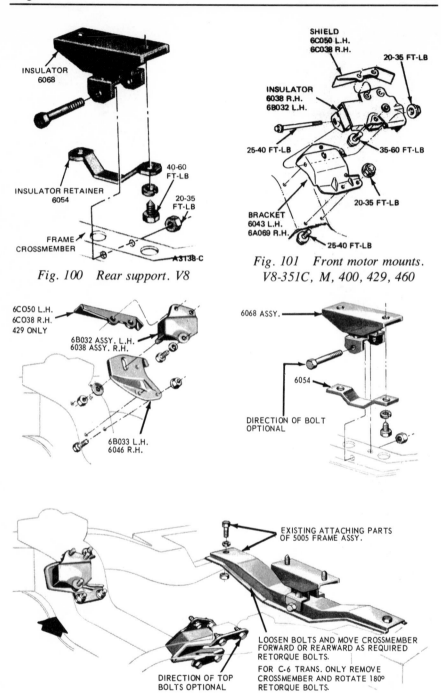

Fig. 100   Rear support. V8

Fig. 101   Front motor mounts.
V8-351C, M, 400, 429, 460

Fig. 102   Engine supports. V8-390

V8–351C, M, 400, 429, 460
Front

1. Bock the rear wheels, set the parking brake and raise the front of the car and support it properly on stands.
2. Place a jack with a block of wood under the front of the oil pan and raise the engine just enough to support the engine.
3. Remove the nut and bolt that attaches the front support insulator to the lower support bracket, Fig. 101.
4. Remove the bolts attaching the support insulator and heat shield (where used) to the engine block. Replace the insulator on one side before proceeding to the other side.

Rear

1. Remove the insulator assembly to crossmember attaching bolts and nuts, Fig. 100.
2. Raise the transmission with a jack to obtain clearance at the transmission extension housing. Then remove the retainer and insulator assembly mounting bolts and washers.
3. Remove the insulator assembly and retainer.

V8–390
Front

1. On a car with automatic transmission, remove the transmission oil cooler inlet and outlet tubes from the retaining bracket on the engine block.
2. Remove the insulator to inter-mediate support bracket lock nut. If only one support is being removed, loosen the other support.
3. Using a jack and a block of wood placed under the oil pan, raise the engine just enough to allow clearance for removal of the insulator.
4. Remove the insulator to engine locking bolts and remove the insulator, Fig. 102.

Rear

1. Remove the attaching bolts, nuts, washers and insulator retainer.
2. Raise the engine slightly to gain access and remove the insulator assembly.

TIMING CHAIN COVER REMOVAL/TIMING CHAIN REPLACEMENT

If the timing chain cover of your Ford is leaking oil, you can fix it with the help we will be giving you. Removing the cover will enable you to replace a worn gasket or seal. Once the timing chain cover has been removed, you will have easy access to the timing chain, in the event it has snapped or jumped timing because of too much stretch or worn gear teeth.

Six Cylinder

1. Drain the cooling system into a suitable pan.
2. If car has an automatic transmission, disconnect oil cooler lines from the radiator and cap them to prevent fluid loss.
3. Disconnect the radiator upper hose at the thermostat housing and the lower hose at the water pump

and remove the radiator.

4. If car has air conditioning, remove condenser attaching bolts and lay it to one side with all lines attached.

5. Remove compressor drive belt.

6. If car has power steering, loosen power steering pump and remove drive belt. Position pump and mounting bracket out of the way with lines connected.

7. Remove the fan and alternator drive belts. Remove the alternator adjusting arm bolt and swing the arm out of the way.

8. Remove the fan, spacer and pulley.

9. Remove accessory drive pulley from crankshaft damper, if so equipped, and remove the crankshaft damper using a simple puller.

10. Remove the oil level dipstick.

11. Remove the front timing cover and drive belt idler pulley assembly, if so equipped, and discard the gasket.

12. Raise the car and support it properly and drain the engine oil.

13. Disconnect the starter cable at the starter and remove the starter.

14. Remove engine front support insulator to intermediate support bracket nuts on both supports. Remove engine rear support insulator to crossmember bolt and insulator to transmission extension housing bolts. Raise transmission and remove the support insulator and lower the transmission to the crossmember.

15. Raise the engine with a suitable jack and place 2″ thick blocks of wood between front support in-

sulators and intermediate support brackets.

16. Remove the oil pan.

17. In order to replace the camshaft gear, the camshaft must be removed. This procedure is best left to a skilled mechanic.

V8–302, 351W

1. Drain the cooling system and the crankcase into suitable containers.

2. On cars equipped with a fan shroud, remove the shroud attaching bolts and position the shroud rearward.

3. Remove the bolts attaching the fan and spacer to the water pump and remove the fan and spacer or fan clutch from the water pump shaft and remove the fan shroud, if so equipped.

4. If car is air conditioned, remove the drive belt and idler pulley bracket.

5. Remove the alternator and drive belt.

6. If car has power steering, remove the pump and drive belt.

7. Remove the water pump pulley.

8. Disconnect the heater hose, radiator hose and by-pass hose at the water pump.

9. Remove the crankshaft pulley from the damper and remove the damper attaching bolt and washer. Install a puller, Fig. 103, and remove the damper.

10. Disconnect the fuel pump outlet line from the pump and remove the fuel pump and lay it aside with the flex line attached.

11. Remove the oil dipstick.

12. Remove the oil pan to timing

UNIVERSAL
PULLER

A3248-A

Fig. 103   Removing vibration damper

chain cover bolts and, using a thin knife, cut the pan gasket flush with the engine block surface prior to separating the timing cover from the engine.

13. Remove the timing chain cover and water pump as an assembly.

14. Before removing the timing chain, crank the engine to line up the valve timing marks, Fig. 104.

15. Remove the camshaft sprocket cap screw and washers and fuel pump eccentric and slide both sprockets and timing chain forward and remove them as an assembly.

V8–351C, M, & V8–400

1. Drain the cooling system into a suitable pan and disconnect the battery ground cable.

2. Remove the fan shroud attaching bolts.

3. Remove the fan and spacer from the water pump shaft.

TIMING MARKS

Fig. 104   Valve timing marks.
V8-302, 351W

4. If car is air conditioned, loosen the lower idler pulley and remove the belt.

5. Loosen the alternator and remove the belt.

6. If car has power steering, loosen the pump and remove the belt.

7. Remove the water pump pulley.

8. Remove the alternator to water pump bracket and position alternator out of the way.

9. Remove power steering pump bracket from the water pump and head and position power steering pump out of the way, if so equipped.

10. Remove air conditioning compressor to water pump bracket and lower idler pulley, if so equipped.

123

A3250—A

*Fig. 105   Valve timing marks.
V8-351C, M, 400*

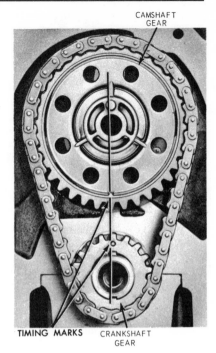

CAMSHAFT
GEAR

TIMING MARKS   CRANKSHAFT
GEAR

*Fig. 106   Valve timing marks.
V8-390*

11. Remove heater hose and lower radiator hose from water pump.
12. Remove crankshaft pulley from damper and remove damper bolt. Attach puller and remove damper.
13. Remove timing pointer.
14. Remove bolts attaching front cover and water pump to engine and remove cover and water pump as an assembly.
15. Disconnect fuel pump outlet line from fuel pump. Remove fuel pump attaching bolt and lay pump to one side with flex line attached.
16. Remove crankshaft front oil slinger.
17. Crank engine to line up valve timing marks, Fig. 105.
18. Remove camshaft sprocket cap

screw, washer and two piece fuel pump eccentric and slide both sprockets and chain forward and remove them as an assembly.

V8–390

1. Drain the cooling system into a suitable pan.
2. Disconnect the radiator upper hose at the thermostat housing and the lower hose at the water pump.
3. If car has automatic transmission, disconnect the oil cooler lines from the radiator and plug them to prevent fluid loss.
4. Remove the radiator.
5. Disconnect the heater hose at the water pump and remove the hose

from the choke housing clamp.
Slide the water pump by-pass hose
clamp toward the engine.

6. If car has power steering, unfasten
the pump bracket mounting bolts
and position the pump to one side
with the lines attached.

7. If car is air conditioned, remove
compressor mounting bolts and
position compressor out of way
with lines attached.

8. Loosen alternator mounting bolts,
remove drive belt and remove the
alternator support bracket bolts at
the water pump and move the
brackets out of the way. Remove
the water pump and fan assembly.

9. If air conditioned, unfasten condenser and position it forward
with lines attached. Remove
compressor drive belt and accessory drive pulley, if so equipped.

10. Remove bolt and washer from end
of crankshaft and remove pulley.
Then remove crankshaft damper
using a simple puller.

11. Disconnect carburetor fuel line at
the fuel pump.

12. Remove fuel pump and lay the
pump to one side with the flex line
attached.

13. Remove the crankshaft sleeve.
Remove screws attaching front
cover to engine and oil pan. Using
a thin knife, cut oil pan gasket
flush to engine block face prior to
separating cover from block.
Then remove front cover.

14. Crank engine to line up valve timing marks as shown in Fig. 106.

15. Remove camshaft sprocket bolt
and the fuel pump eccentric.

16. Timing chain and sprockets can
now be slid off for replacement.

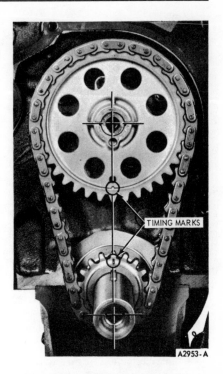

Fig. 107   Valve timing marks.
V8-429, 460

V8–429, 460

1. Drain cooling system and crankcase into suitable containers.

2. Remove bolts attaching fan
shroud to radiator and remove
bolts attaching fan to water pump
shaft. Remove fan and fan
shroud.

3. Disconnect radiator upper and
lower hoses at engine and disconnect transmission cooler lines at
radiator, if so equipped.

4. Remove radiator upper support
and remove radiator.

5. Loosen alternator and air conditioner idler pulley, if so equipped, and remove drive belts with
water pump pulley.

6. Remove air conditioner compressor support, if so equipped.
7. Remove crankshaft pulley from damper.
8. Remove bolt attaching damper and remove damper with a puller.
9. Loosen by-pass hose at water pump and disconnect heater return tube at water pump.
10. Disconnect and plug fuel inlet line at fuel pump. Disconnect fuel line to carburetor at fuel pump and remove fuel pump.
11. Remove bolts attaching front timing cover to engine and using a sharp knife, cut the oil pan seal flush with the engine block prior to separating the cover from the engine.
12. Remove front cover and water pump as an assembly.
13. Crank engine to line up valve timing marks, Fig. 107.
14. Remove camshaft sprocket cap screw, washer and two piece fuel pump eccentric.
15. Slide chain and sprockets forward and remove them as an assembly.

OIL PAN REMOVAL

Six Cylinder

1. Drain the engine oil and the cooling system into suitable containers.
2. Disconnect the radiator upper hose at the thermostat housing and the lower hose at the radiator. Disconnect automatic transmission oil cooler lines at the radiator and cap them to prevent fluid loss.
3. Remove the radiator.
4. If car is air conditioned, remove the condenser attaching bolts and position the condenser to one side with the lines attached.
5. Raise the car and support it properly on stands.
6. Disconnect the starter cable at the starter and remove the starter.
7. Remove the engine front support insulator to intermediate support bracket nuts on both supports. Remove the engine rear support insulator to crossmember bolt and insulator to transmission extension housing bolts. Raise the transmission and remove the support insulator and then lower tower the transmission to the crossmember.
8. Raise the engine with a suitable jack and place 3″ thick blocks of wood between both front support insulators and intemediate support brackets.
9. Remove the stabilizer bar.
10. Remove the oil pan attaching bolts and allow the pan to rest on the crossmember. Remove the oil pump attaching bolts and place the pump in the bottom of the pan. Rotate the crankshaft as required to remove the oil pan.

V8–302, 351W

1. Remove the oil level dipstick.
2. Unbolt the fan shroud from the radiator and position the shroud back over the fan.
3. Raise the car and support it properly on stands.
4. Drain the engine oil into a suitable pan.
5. Disconnect the stabilizer bar from the chassis.

6. Remove the engine front support through bolts and raise the engine and place blocks of wood between the front supports and the frame brackets.
7. If car has an automatic transmission, disconnect the oil cooler lines at the radiator. Plug lines to prevent loss of fluid.
8. Unbolt the oil pan and lower the pan onto the crossmember.
9. Remove the oil pump pickup tube and screen from the oil pump and then rotate the crankshaft to provide clearance and remove the oil pan.

V8–351C, 351M, 400

1. Remove the oil level dipstick.
2. Unbolt the fan shroud and position the shroud back over the fan.
3. Raise the car and support it properly on stands.
4. Drain the engine oil into a suitable pan.
5. Disconnect the starter cable and remove the starter.
6. If car has an automatic transmission, disconnect oil cooler lines from radiator and plug them to prevent loss of fluid.
7. Disconnect the sway bar from the chassis to provide clearance.
8. Remove the engine front support through bolts and raise the engine and place blocks of wood between engine supports and frame brackets.
9. Remove the oil pan bolts and lower and remove the oil pan.

V8–390

1. Raise the car and support it prop-

erly on stands.
2. Drain the engine oil into a suitable pan.
3. If equipped with air conditioning, remove the fan shroud from the radiator and position it over the fan.
4. Disconnect the stabilizer bar at the connecting links and pull the ends down.
5. Remove engine front support insulator to intermediate support bracket nuts and lock washers. Install a block of wood on a floor jack and position the jack under the front edge of the oil pan.
6. Raise the engine about 1¼" and insert a 1" thick block of wood between the insulators and the frame crossmember. Remove the floor jack.
7. Remove the oil pan attaching bolts and lower the pan to the crossmember.
8. Rotate the crankshaft as necessary to gain clearance to remove the oil pan.

V8–429, 460

1. Disconnect the battery ground cable to prevent accidental shorts.
2. Unbolt the fan shroud from the radiator and position it back over the fan.
3. Raise the car and support it properly on stands.
4. Drain the engine oil into a suitable pan.
5. Disconnect the sway bar and move it forward on the struts.
6. Remove the front engine support through bolts.
7. Using a floor jack and with a

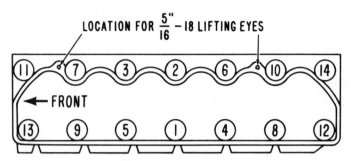

Fig. 108   Cylinder head tightening sequence. Six cylinder

block of wood placed under the front edge of the oil pan, raise the engine just enough to enable you to place blocks of wood 1¼" thick between the engine mounts and the brackets. Then lower the engine onto the blocks of wood and remove the jack.

8. Remove the oil filter.
9. Unbolt and remove the oil pan. It may be necessary to rotate the crankshaft slightly to provide clearance between the pan and the counterweights or throws on the crankshaft.

VALVE ARRANGEMENT

Front to Rear

6-240	E-I-E-I-E-I-E-I-E-I
302, 351, 429 Right	I-E-I-E-I-E-I-E
302,351,429 Left	E-I-E-I-E-I-E-I
390	E-I-E-I-I-E-I-E
400, 460 Right	I-E-I-E-I-E-I-E
400, 460 Left	E-I-E-I-E-I-E-I

E-Exhaust   ·I-Intake

CYLINDER HEAD REMOVAL

If after taking a compression test,

you have established that a valve grinding job is necessary, you can remove the cylinder heads yourself with the help of this book, and take them to a local automotive machine shop to have the valve job done. By doing this labor yourself, you will probably save enough to pay for the valve job.

Here is how you can get the cylinder heads off the engine, and save money.

Six Cylinder

1. Drain the cooling system into a suitable pan.
2. Disconnect radiator upper hose and heater hose from coolant outlet housing.
3. Disconnect radiator upper hose and heater hose from coolant outlet housing.
3. Disconnect temperature wire from sending unit.
4. Disconnect and remove carburetor fuel inlet line and distributor vacuum lines.
5. Remove accelerator cable return spring and disconnect cable housing bracket from cylinder head and position cable and bracket out of way.
6. If car has automatic transmission,

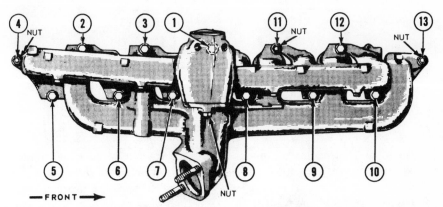

Fig. 109   Manifold tightening sequence. Six cylinder

disconnect kickdown rod at bellcrank.

7. Pull crankcase ventilator valve out of valve cover and disconnect hose from manifold and remove valve and hose.

8. If car has power brakes, disconnect vacuum line at manifold.

9. Remove valve rocker arm cover and loosen rocker arm stud nuts so rocker arms can be rotated to one side.

10. Remove the push rods and place them in a rack in sequence so they may be returned to their original positions.

11. Disconnect spark plug wires from spark plugs making sure they are marked so they can be properly replaced.

12. Disconnect exhaust pipe from manifold and discard gasket.

13. Remove cylinder head bolts and lift off cylinder head. Place head on blocks of wood to avoid damage.

14. When replacing head, tighten bolts in sequence as shown in Fig. 108 and to the tightness listed in

the chart. Manifolds should be tightened in the sequence shown in Fig. 109 and to the tightness listed in the chart.

V8–Except 390

1. Drain the cooling system into a suitable pan.

2. On V8–302 engines, disconnect the choke heat chamber air inlet hose at the inlet tube near the right (passenger side) valve rocker arm cover.

3. Remove the air cleaner assembly, crankcase ventilation hose and intake duct assembly.

4. Disconnect the accelerator rod or cable from the carburetor and/or manifold brackets. Remove the accelerator retracting spring.

5. If so equipped, disconnect the automatic transmission and power brake booster vacuum lines at the intake manifold.

6. Mark and disconnect wires from the ignition coil so they may be returned to original positions upon reassembly.

129

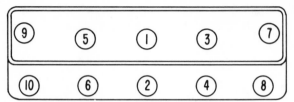

Fig. 110   Cylinder head tightening. V8

7. Remove Thermactor air pump by-pass valve and air supply hoses.

8. Disconnect spark plug wires from spark plugs after properly marking them for reassembly purposes. Do not pull on the wires to remove them. Grasp them down at the boot on the spark plug and twist and pull to remove them. Remove

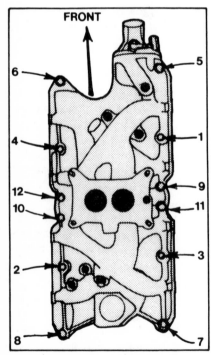

Fig. 111   Intake manifold tightening sequence. V8-302

the wires from the harness brackets on the valve rocker arm covers. Remove the distributor cap and spark plug wires as an assembly.

9. At the rear of the manifold, remove the Exhaust Gas Recirculation vacuum amplifier.

10. On V8–302 engines, remove the carburetor fuel inlet line and the choke heat tube.

11. Disconnect distributor vacuum hoses and after marking relative position of rotor to distributor housing and distributor housing to manifold, remove the distributor hold-down bolt and remove the distributor.

12. Disconnect hoses from thermostat housing on manifold and disconnect temperature sending unit wire from sending unit.

13. Disconnect crankcase ventilation hose at valve rocker arm cover.

14. Mark and disconnect any remaining wires and vacuum hoses.

15. Unbolt and remove the intake manifold and carburetor as an assembly. It may be necessary to pry the manifold away from the cylinder heads so use care to avoid damage to the gasket surfaces.

16. Remove valve rocker arm covers.

17. Disconnect exhaust pipes from exhaust manifolds.

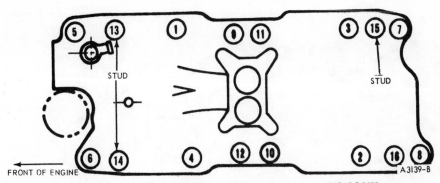

Fig. 112   Intake manifold tightening sequence. V8-351W

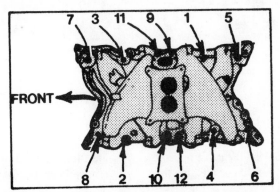

*Fig. 113   Intake manifold tightening
sequence. V8-351C, M, 400*

18. Disconnect and remove as necessary, the alternator, air conditioning compressor and power steering pump.

19. Loosen the rocker arm stud nuts on fulcrum bolts so the rocker arms can be rotated to the side. Remove the push rods in sequence and place them in a rack so they can be returned to their original positions. On V8–302 engines, remove the exhaust valve stem caps.

20. Unbolt the cylinder heads and carefully lift them off the engine block. Place heads on blocks of wood to avoid damage.

21. When replacing the heads, tighten the bolts in the sequence shown in Fig. 110 and to the tightness listed in the chart.

22. When replacing the intake manifold, tighten the bolts in the sequence shown in Figs. 111 through 115 and to the tightness listed in the chart.

V8-390

1. Drain the cooling system into a suitable pan. Remove the hood and the carburetor air cleaner assembly.

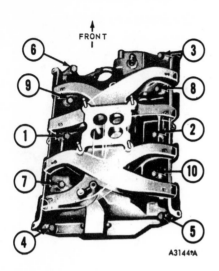

Fig. 114   Intake manifold tightening
            sequence. V8-390

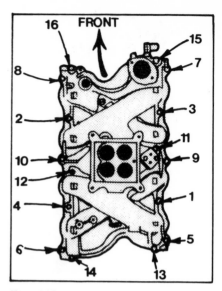

Fig. 115   Intake manifold tightening
            sequence. V8-429, 460

2. Disconnect the accelerator cable at the carburetor and remove the return spring and the cable bracket from the manifold and position the cable and bracket out of the way.

3. If car has automatic transmission, remove the kickdown rod retracting spring and disconnect the kickdown rod at the carburetor and the spacer vacuum line.

4. Disconnect coil leads at the distributor and disconnect the oil pressure wire at the sending unit.

5. Disconnect spark plug wires from spark plugs after marking them so they can be returned to their correct positions. Remove the wires from the harness brackets on the valve covers.

6. Remove the distributor cap and spark plug wires as an assembly and disconnect vacuum hoses at distributor.

7. Disconnect carburetor fuel line at

the fuel filter. Remove the choke air heat tube and the heat chamber air inlet tube. Disconnect brake booster vacuum line at manifold and at the flex hose and remove the vacuum line.

8. Mark distributor rotor position on distributor housing and mark distributor housing position in manifold and remove distributor.

9. Disconnect radiator upper hose at the thermostat housing and the heater hoses from the intake manifold. Disconnect water temperature wire at the sending unit. Disconnect heater hose at water pump and remove it from the choke housing bracket.

10. Loosen clamp on water pump by-pass hose and slide it toward the water pump.

11. Remove crankcase ventilator

valve (PCV) from right valve rocker cover.

12. Disconnect any air lines and hoses for accessibility.

13. Remove the valve rocker arm covers.

14. Crank engine until number one cylinder is at TDC of cmpression stroke. Rotate the damper an additional 45 degrees (identified by XX on damper).

15. On right head start at the most rearward cylinder and loosen the rocker arm shaft support bolts in sequence, two turns at a time. After all bolts are loosened, remove rocker arm shaft assembly and oil baffle plate.

16. On left head, start at the front cylinder and loosen the bolts in sequence two turns at a time. After all bolts are loosened, remove the rocker arm shaft assembly.

17. Remove the valve push rods and place them in a rack in sequence for proper installation.

18. Remove the intake manifold attaching bolts. Install standard eye bolts with $5/16$ x 18 threads in the left front and right rear rocker arm cover screw holes and attach a lifting device to these eye bolts.

19. Lift the intake manifold off the engine and remove gaskets and seals.

20. Unbolt and remove cylinder head.

21. When replacing cylinder head, tighten the bolts in the sequence shown in Fig. 110 and to the tightness listed in the chart.

22. When replacing the intake manifold, tighten the bolts in the sequence shown in Fig. 114 and to the tightness listed in the chart.

ENGINE REMOVAL

When an engine has outlived its usefulness and a complete overhaul is indicated, the cost can be devastating. But even in these circumstances, we have a tip that can still help you to save money. A perfectly good engine may be available at a local salvage yard. This engine although very probably removed from a wrecked Ford, may nonetheless be in good running condition. The damage may have had no affect on the engine itself. Most reputable salvage yards will even run the engine for you and many will provide some warranty. Be sure you fully understand any warranty and its conditions. If you are successful in locating your engine at a salvage yard you will be able to save hundreds of dollars from the price of a new engine. You can rent a hoist and any necessary jacks from local rent-all centers at low prices, so, with you providing the labor, here is how to remove your engine. (To install the replacement engine, simply reverse the steps).

Six Cylinder

1. Open the hood and scribe the outline of the hood hinges on the bottom side of the hood, then remove the hood assembly.

2. Drain the cooling system and engine oil into suitable containers.

3. Disconnect the crankcase ventilation hose and remove the air cleaner assembly.

4. Disconnect the battery ground cable to prevent accidental shorts.

5. Disconnect the radiator upper

hose at the thermostat housing and the radiator lower hose at the water pump.

6. If car has automatic transmission, disconnect the oil cooler lines from the radiator and plug them to prevent loss of fluid.

7. Remove the radiator, fan, spacer, belt and pulley.

8. Disconnect heater hoses from the water pump and the engine block.

9. Disconnect alternator wires from alternator and starter cable from the starter.

10. Disconnect accelerator control cable from the carburetor.

11. If car has air conditioning, remove compressor from its mounting bracket and position it out of way leaving lines attached.

12. Disconnect fuel flex line at the fuel pump line and cap line.

13. Disconnect all wires from ignition coil (mark them for proper installation).

14. Disconnect wires from oil pressure and temperature sending units.

15. Remove the starter.

16. If car has a manual shift transmission, disconnect clutch retracting spring. Disconnect clutch equalizer shaft and arm bracket at the underbody rail and remove the arm bracket and equalizer shaft.

17. Raise the car and support it properly on stands. Remove the flywheel or converter housing upper attaching bolts.

18. Disconnect the exhaust pipe at the exhaust manifold. Loosen the exhaust pipe clamp and slide it off the bracket on the engine.

19. Disconnect the engine mounts at the underbody brackets.

20. Remove the flywheel or converter housing cover.

21. If car has a manual shift transmission, remove the flywheel housing lower attaching bolts.

22. If car has automatic transmission, disconnect the converter from the flywheel and remove the converter housing lower attaching bolts.

23. Lower the car. Support the transmission with a suitable jack.

24. Attach the engine lifting device and carefully lift the engine out of car. Be sure the converter is secured to transmission so it will not fall out when engine is removed.

V8 Engine

1. Drain the cooling system and the engine oil into suitable containers.

2. Trace outline of hood hinges on bottom side of hood, for poper installation, and remove hood assembly.

3. Disconnect the battery and alternator ground cables from the engine.

4. Remove the air cleaner assembly and intake duct hose, where used.

5. Disconnect radiator upper hose from thermostat housing and the radiator lower hose from the water pump.

6. If car has automatic transmission, disconnect oil cooler lines from radiator and cap them to prevent fluid loss.

7. Remove the bolts attaching the fan shroud to the radiator, if so equipped.

8. Remove the radiator, fan, spacer, belt, pulley and fan shroud.

9. Disconnect heater hoses from the water pump and intake manifold.

10. Disconnect accelerator rod from the carburetor.

11. Remove alternator bolts and position alternator out of way.

12. Disconnect oil pressure sender wire from the sender and the flex fuel line at the fuel tank line and plug the fuel line.

13. If car has automatic transmission, disconnect throttle valve vacuum line from intake manifold and disconnect transmission filler tube bracket from engine.

14. If car has manual shift transmission, disconnect shift rod and the retracting spring at the shift rod stud.

15. If car has air conditioning, remove the compressor from the engine.

16. If car has power steering, disconnect the pump bracket from the cylinder head, remove the drive belt and position the pump out of the way in a manner that will not allow the fluid to drain out of it.

17. If car has power brakes, disconnect the brake vacuum line from the intake manifold.

18. Disconnect temperature sender wire from sender unit.

19. Remove the flywheel or converter housing to engine upper bolts.

20. Disconnect primary wire from ignition coil. Remove the wire harness from the left rocker arm cover and position wires out of way.

21. Disconnect engine ground strap from engine block.

22. Raise front of car and support it properly on stands.

23. Disconnect starter cable from star-ter and remove the starter.

24. Disconnect exhaust pipes from exhaust manifolds and disconnect engine mount insulators from the brackets on the frame.

25. If car has manual shift transmission, remove the bolts attaching the clutch equalizer bar to frame rail and equalizer from engine block. Remove the remaining flywheel housing to engine bolts.

26. If car has automatic transmission, disconnect cooler lines from retainer and remove converter housing inspection cover. Disconnect flywheel from converter and secure converter in the housing. Then remove the remaining converter housing to engine bolts.

27. Lower the car and support the transmission.

28. Attach suitable lifting device to engine and raise engine carefully. Be sure all wires and hoses are disconnected and carefully pull engine away from transmission and lift it out of the engine compartment.

TIGHTENING BOLTS

When replacing engine components, it is important to use a torque wrench to establish the correct bolt tightness as listed in the following chart. Too loose may be less damaging than too tight but in fact, either can lead to engine damage. Spark plugs not tightened sufficiently will run hot, head bolts not tightened properly will cause a gasket leak or if an attempt is made to overtighten a bolt it will most likely shear off (break) and lead to more work in removing the broken piece. So, whether you own a torque wrench or borrow one, use it only for the purpose it was made for and it will maintain its accuracy for a longer time.

ENGINE TIGHTENING SPECIFICATIONS*

★ Torque specifications are for clean and lightly lubricated threads only. Dry or dirty threads produce increased friction which prevents accurate measurement of tightness.

Year	Engine	Spark Plugs Ft. Lbs.	Cylinder Head Bolts Ft. Lbs.	Intake Manifold Ft. Lbs.	Exhaust Manifold Ft. Lbs.	Rocker Arm Shaft Bracket Ft. Lbs.	Rocker Arm Cover Ft. Lbs.
1970-72	6-240	15–20	70–75	23–28	23–28	—	7–9
1970-72	V8-302	15–20	65–72	23–25	12–16	17–23①	3–5
1970-72	V8-351	15–20	95–100	23–25	18–24	17–23①	3–5
1970-71	V8-390	15–20	80–90	32–35	18–24	40–45	4–7
1971-72	V8-400	15–20	95–105	②	12–16	18–25③	3–5
1970-72	V8-429	15–20	130–140	25–30	28–33	④	5–6
1973	V8-351W	15–20	105–112	23–25	18–24	17–23①	3–5
	V8-351C	15–20	95–105	②	12–22	18–25③	3–5
	V8-400	15–20	95–105	②	12–16	18–25③	3–5
	V8-429, 460	15–20	130–140	25–30	28–33.	18–25③	5–6
1974	V8-351W	15–20	105–112	19–27	18–24	17–23①	3–5
	V8-351C	15–20	95–105	⑤	12–22	18–25③	3–5
	V8-400	15–20	95–105	⑤	12–16	18–25③	3–5
	V8-460	15–20	130–140	22–32	28–33	18–25③	5–6
1975-76	V8-351	10–15	95–105	②	18–24	18–25③	3–5
	V8-400	10–15	95–105	②	18–24	18–25③	3–5
	V8-460	10–15	130–140	25–30	28–33	18–25③	5–6
1977	V8-351	10–15	95–105	⑥	18–24	18–25③	5–6
	V8-400	10–15	95–105	⑥	18–24	18–25③	5–6
	V8-460	10–15	130–140	22–32	28–33	18–25③	5–6

①—Rocker arm stud nut.
②—5/16" bolts 21–25 ft. lbs. 3/8" bolts 27–33 ft. lbs. 1/4" bolts 6–9 ft. lbs.
③—Fulcrum bolt to cylinder head.
④—1970 rocker arm stud to cylinder head; 65–75 ft. lbs. 1971-72 fulcrum bolt to cylinder head; 18–25 ft. lbs.
⑤—5/16" bolts, 22–32; 3/8" bolts, 17–25; 1/4" bolts, 6–9.
⑥—5/16" bolts, 19–25; 3/8" bolts, 22–32.

Clutch, Transmission & Propeller Shaft

This section will provide the help you need in making some minor adjustments to the clutch and transmission linkage, as well as providing some, more complex procedures, for removing transmissions, should that be necessary. Don't be frightened about removing these units. We'll be helping you and any jacks you might need can usually be rented at local rent-all centers. You can save a lot of money by doing the labor yourself. When needed, replacement transmissions can be located at local salvage yards. These units were removed from cars that were wrecked but such wrecks may have had no effect at all on the condition of a transmission. The reduced price you pay for a serviceable transmission at a salvage yard will help you to keep your car running and avoid the expense of buying another car. When dealing with the salvage yard, be sure you fully understand any warranty that accompanies the unit you are buying.

CLUTCH PEDAL ADJUSTMENT

If you are having trouble shifting gears, or if there is a gear grinding or clashing while shifting, the cause may well be a clutch in need of adjustment. This adjustment is quite simple and here is how you can do it.

1970-72

1. Working beneath the car, disconnect the clutch return spring from the release lever, Fig. 116
2. Loosen the release lever rod locknut and adjusting nut.
3. Move the clutch release lever rearward until the release bearing lightly contacts the clutch pressure plate release fingers.
4. Adjust the rod length until the rod seats in the release lever pocket.
5. Insert a feeler gauge or drill .194" thick between the adjusting nut and the swivel sleeve. Then tighten the adjusting nut against the gauge.
6. Tighten the locknut against the adjusting nut, being careful not to disturb the adjustment and remove the feeler gauge or drill.
7. Install the clutch return spring and check the free play at the pedal. With the engine running, the free play should be ⅞" to 1⅛".

CLUTCH REPLACEMENT

If your car feels like it has no power, don't overlook the possibility that the clutch is worn. Remember, the clutch has a facing or lining similar to that used on brakes. So, if this is your trouble, or if you can't keep the clutch adjusted properly, the clutch may need replacing. You can do this job yourself and save the labor charges. These parts can be purchased at your local automotive parts supply store. Replace the clutch as follows:

1. Raise the car and support it properly on stands.
2. If used, disconnect any electrical

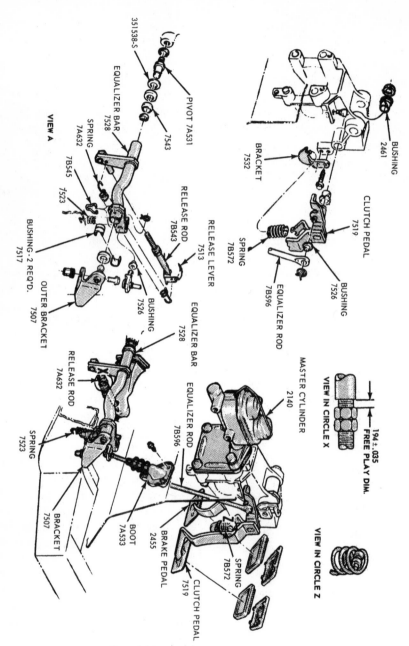

Fig. 116   Clutch linkage adjustment

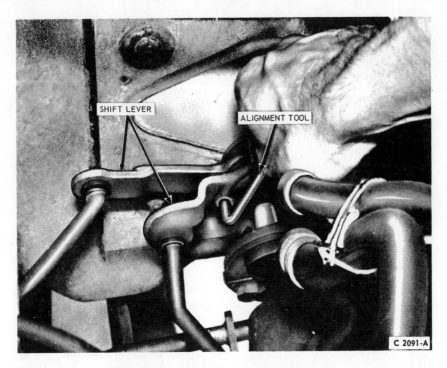

Fig. 117   Gearshift linkage adjustment

leads from transmission.

3. Mark the driveshaft so that it can be installed in its same relative position. Disconnect the shaft from the rear universal joint flange.

4. Slide the front of the shaft out of the transmission extension housing and off the transmission output shaft.

5. Disconnect speedometer cable from extension housing.

6. If car has a column mounted gear shift, disconnect the shift rods from the shift levers at the transmission.

7. If car has a floor mounted shift lever, remove the shift selector assembly from the extension housing.

8. Support the transmission and engine suitable jacks and remove the nuts attaching the engine rear support to the crossmember.

9. Remove the bolts attaching the crossmember to the frame and remove the crossmember.

10. While supporting the transmission, remove the bolts attaching the transmission to the flywheel housing and carefully move the transmission rearward until the input shaft clears the flywheel housing. If necessary, lower engine a bit to gain clearance for transmission removal and remove transmission.

11. Disconnect clutch release lever retaining spring from the lever.

12. Remove the starter cable from the

starter and remove the starter.

13. Remove the bolts securing engine rear plate to the front lower part of the flywheel housing. Remove housing lower cover, if so equipped.

14. Remove bolts attaching flywheel housing to engine.

15. Move the housing back far enough to clear the pressure plate then move it to the right to free the pivot from the clutch equalizer bar. Be careful not to disturb the clutch linkage and assist spring.

16. Loosen the six pressure plate attaching bolts evenly to release the spring tension and avoid distortion of the cover. If the same pressure plate is going to be installed, mark the cover and flywheel so it can be returned to its same relative position.

17. Remove the attaching bolts and the clutch pressure plate and disc from the flywheel.

SYNCHRO-MESH TRANSMISSION LINKAGE ADJUSTMENT

1970-72 Column Shift

1. Place gear shift lever in the Neutral position.

2. Loosen the two gear shift rod adjustment nuts.

3. Check that the shift levers on the transmission are in Neutral position.

4. Insert a $3/16''$ diameter rod through the first and reverse gear shift lever, the second and third gear shift lever and both holes in the lower casting, Fig. 117

5. Tighten the two gear shift rod adjustment nuts.

6. Remove the alignment tool from the levers, start the engine and check operation of the shift lever in all positions.

SYNCHRO-MESH TRANSMISSION REMOVAL

If the transmission is in need of overhaul, the cost will be rather high. Consider the possibility of removing the transmission yourself and buying a replacement unit at your local salvage yard. Such units, although removed from wrecked cars, may still have many thousands of miles left in them. Just be sure you fully understand any warranty that may accompany the purchase of such a unit. Since you will not be able to see the replacement transmission operating, we suggest you remove the cover on the transmission and visually inspect the condition of the gears.

1. Raise the car and support it properly on stands.

2. Where used, disconnect any electrical leads from transmission.

3. Mark the driveshaft so that it can be installed in its same relative position. Disconnect the driveshaft from the rear universal joint flange.

4. Slide the front of the driveshaft out of the transmission extension housing and off the transmission output shaft.

5. Disconnect speedometer cable from extension housing.

6. Disconnect the shift rods from the shift levers at the transmission.

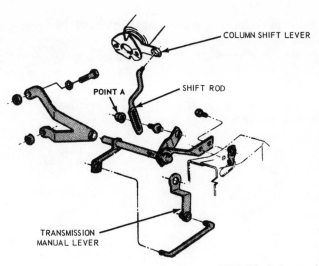

COLUMN SHIFT LEVER

SHIFT ROD

POINT A

TRANSMISSION
MANUAL LEVER

Fig. 118   Automatic linkage adjustment. 1970-75 Column shift

7. Disconnect the parking brake cable from the equalizer lever and separate the lever from the crossmember.
8. Remove the bolts that secure the transmission extension housing to the engine rear support.
9. Raise the rear of the engine high enough to remove the weight from the crossmember.
10. Support the transmission with a suitable jack and remove the transmission from the flywheel housing.
11. Move the transmission rearward until the input shaft clears the flywheel housing.

AUTOMATIC TRANSMISSION LINKAGE ADJUSTMENT

1970-75 Column Shift

1. Place the selector lever in the D position tight against the D stop.
2. Loosen the shift rod adjusting nut at point "A" in Fig. 118
3. Shift the manual lever at the transmission into the D position.
4. Make sure the selector lever has not moved from the D position and then tighten the adjusting nut shown at point "A".

1970-72 Floor Shift

1. Position the transmission selector lever in the D position.
2. Raise the car and support it properly on stands and loosen the manual lever shift rod retaining nut, Fig. 119. Move the transmission manual lever to the D position.
3. With the transmission selector lever and the manual lever in the D position, tighten the attaching nut.

141

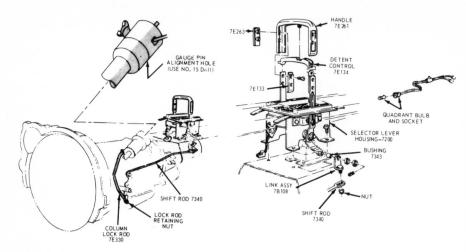

Fig. 119   Automatic linkage adjustment. 1970-72 floor shift

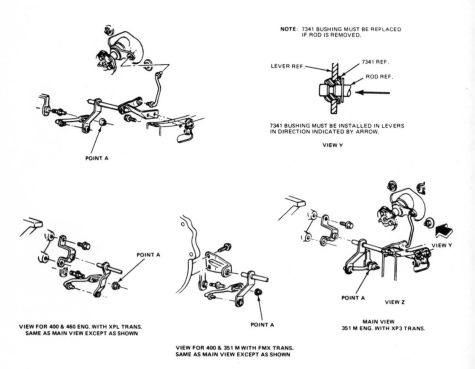

Fig. 120   Automatic linkage adjustment. 1976-77 column shift

1976-77 Column Shift

1. Place the selector lever in Drive position tight against the D stop.
2. Loosen the shift rod adjusting nut at point "A", Fig. 120.
3. Shift the transmission manual lever into the D position.
4. Make sure the shift selector has not moved from the D position and tighten the nut at point "A".

AUTOMATIC TRANSMISSION REMOVAL

Should the automatic transmission in your Ford be in need of a complete overhaul, don't let that alone influence your decision to dispose of the car. Units in good condition may be available at local salvage yards. Although these units were removed from wrecked cars, the transmission may still be in good condition, and they can be bought rather cheaply. Be sure you fully understand the terms of any warranty that accompanies the sale of such a unit.

Since you will not be able to see the transmission operating, we suggest you remove the pan to see if there is any evidence of clutch failure.

On some models, it will be necessary to remove the two upper converter housing to engine bolts before raising the car. Otherwise, proceed as follows:

1. Raise the car and support it properly on stands.
2. Drain the transmission oil pan and the converter. The converter drain plugs are accessible after removing the converter housing access cover.
3. Disconnect the driveshaft at the rear axle. Mark the relationship of the shaft with the axle flange so it can be reinstalled in the same position.
4. Remove starter motor.
5. Remove converter to flywheel attaching bolts.
6. Disconnect oil cooler lines, speedometer cable, vacuum hose, electrical leads and linkage from transmisssion.
7. If necessary to gain clearance, disconnect exhaust pipes from manifolds.
8. Disconnect parking brake cable at equalizer.
9. Support transmission with a suitable jack, and remove crossmember.
10. Support engine with a suitable jack and remove converter housing to engine bolts.
11. Be sure transmission is now free, and carefully move transmission rearward until clear of engine and lower it away from the car.

PROPELLER SHAFT REMOVAL

In order to be able to remove a clutch, transmission or maybe even an engine, it will be necessary for you to first remove the propeller shaft or driveshaft, as it sometimes referred to. It is quite simple to do this and here is how to proceed.

1. To maintain drive line balance, mark the relationship of the rear

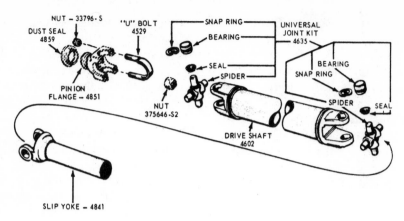

NUT – 33796-S
DUST SEAL 4859
"U" BOLT 4529
SNAP RING
BEARING
UNIVERSAL JOINT KIT 4635
PINION FLANGE – 4851
SEAL
SPIDER
BEARING
SNAP RING
NUT 375646-S2
SPIDER
SEAL
DRIVE SHAFT 4602
SLIP YOKE – 4841

Fig. 121   Propeller shaft details

drive shaft yoke and the axle drive pinion flange so the shaft can be installed in its same relative position.

2. Disconnect the rear U-joint from the companion flange and wrap tape around the loose bearing cups to prevent them from falling off.

3. Pull the driveshaft toward the rear of the car until the yoke clears the transmission extension housing and remove the shaft, Fig. 121.

Trouble Diagnosis Guide

INDEX OF SYMPTOMS

COOLING SYSTEM

COOLANT TEMPERATURE INDICATOR

EXHAUST SYSTEM

CLUTCH & SYNCHRO-MESH TRANSMISSION

BRAKES

SUSPENSION & STEERING

Introduction

The front of this book tells you how to repair and maintain your car. This special Trouble Diagnosis Guide will simplify your tasks still further by telling you *what* symptoms you should be on the lookout for and, once observed, what the symptoms mean. Warning signs almost always precede a breakdown. By using the TDG section of your book you will increase your awareness of the many possible symptoms of car failure that can take you by surprise and cost you big money if neglected. It is easier on the pocketbook to prevent a problem than it is to repair it. So become familiar with the scope of the TDG right now and refer to it often.

In the TDG, we have included 141 symptoms of car trouble, the possible causes of each symptom and the corrective measures to be taken. In our experience, the symptoms listed account for almost 100% of the kinds of repair and maintenance situations you might encounter. You will also notice that many of the corrective measures listed are the very same repair and maintenance operations that are described in the front of the book. In this way you can use the TDG to help you to identify a symptom, to zero in on its cause and to determine its correction. Once you have determined the corrective measure to be taken, you can use the step by step instructions in the front of the book, to perform the necessary task. In this way, repairs are simply and successfully achieved because we are there, at your side, at every step along the way.

For purposes of completeness, the TDG also includes some corrective measures which are best left to the automotive service professional. These are included to help you deal more knowledgeably and confidently with the professional who works on your car.

SPOTTING SYMPTOMS

Try to develop the habit of looking and listening for trouble symptoms. The most obvious symptom is, of course, "my engine won't start". So we will deal with that symptom fully and separately. But short of a car that cannot be started, there are many symptoms that are easy to spot, if you use your senses effectively.

Always examine the ground around your car for fluid leakage. When your hood is up check out the engine for wet spots. Keep your eyes open for a worn tire, an exposed or loose wire or a cracked hose. And by all means, after making sure that all of your instrument panel lamps and gauges are working, be sure to glance at them occasionally.

You should also learn to use your ears to detect strange noises, not noticed before. A rattle or a knock or a ping may be the first sign of a worn part.

Finally, be alert for the smell of fuel, and learn to distinguish it from the smell of brake fluid or coolant or oil. With this in mind, read through the TDG and begin to sharpen your "symptom spotting skills".

STARTING A STALLED ENGINE

When an engine fails to start the chances are that in 90 per cent of the cases, only the ignition system is involved and seldom the fuel system or other miscellaneous reasons. Therefore, if a systematic procedure is followed, the trouble can almost always be found quickly and easily, without the use of special equipment.

To begin with, turn on the ignition switch and if the ammeter shows a slight discharge (or if the telltale lamp lights) it indicates that current is flowing. A glance at the gas gauge will indicate whether or not there is fuel in the tank.

Operate the starter and if the engine turns over freely, both the battery and starter are functioning properly. On the other hand, if the starter action is sluggish, it may be due to a discharged or defective battery or loose, corroded or dirty battery terminals, or a mechanical failure in the starter, starter switch or starter drive. If the starter circuit is okay, skip this phase of the discussion and proceed to ignition.

Starter Circuit Checkout

To determine which part of the starter circuit is at fault, turn on your lights and again operate the starter. Should the lights go out or become dim, the trouble is either in the battery, its connections or its cables. A hydrometer test or the battery should indicate better than 1.250 specific gravity, while a voltmeter, placed across the positive and negative posts, should indicate about 12 volts. If either of these tests prove okay, clean and tighten the battery connections and cable terminals or replace any cable which seems doubtful.

If the lights remain bright; no change whatever, when the starter is operated, the trouble is between the battery and the starter, or the starter switch is at fault, since it is evident that there is no electrical connection between these points. If these connections are clean and tight, it is safe to assume that the starter or starter switch is defective.

Neutral Safety Switch

If the ammeter shows a slight discharge (or if the telltale lamp lights) when the ignition is turned on, but the system goes dead when the starter is turned on, the neutral safety switch may be at fault.

Primary Ignition Checkout

Let's assume that the battery and starter are doing their job, and that fuel is reaching the carburetor, but the car does not start, then the trouble must be somewhere in the ignition circuit. But first, before starting your diagnosis, it is advisable to give the whole system a visual inspection which might uncover obvious things such as broken or disconnected wires etc.

The best way to start tracking down ignition troubles is to begin with the primary circuit since this is where troubles show up most frequently. First remove the distributor cap and block the points open with a piece of cardboard, then turn on the ignition and with a test bulb or voltmeter check to see if there is current at the terminal on the distributor. If you do not get a

reading at this point, the current is cut off somewhere in the connections leading back to the ignition switch. Or it may be that the condenser has an internal short to the ground. This possibility can be eliminated if you can restore current at the distributor terminal by disconnecting the condenser. With the possibility of a bad condenser out of the way, work toward the ignition switch and test for current at each connection until you get to a connection where you get a reading. Between this connection and the distributor lies the trouble.

The foregoing steps in checking the primary circuit should include checking the ignition coil resistor for defects or loose connections. As this is done, bear in mind that while the starter cranks the engine, the resistor is bypassed by the starter switch on most systems. This means that while the circuit through the resistor may be satisfactory, a broken connection or high resistance between the starter switch by-pass terminal and the coil would prevent starting. On the other hand, a satisfactory by-pass circuit might start the engine while the engine would stall immediately upon releasing the ignition switch if there was a defect in the coil resistance circuit.

If, the test equipment shows a current reading at the distributor terminal, it is safe to assume that the trouble is in the unit itself, most likely burned or dirty breaker points. A final positive test for defective breaker points can be made very simply by removing the cardboard from between the points, and positioning the distributor cam by turning the engine to where the points are closed. With the points closed there should be no current at the distributor terminal. If there is current, replace the points.

In an emergency, the points can be cleaned by using the sanded side of a match box, a knife blade, or the sharp edge of a screwdriver to scrape the scale from the contact faces. After cleaning the points, if a gauge is not available to set the gap, a quick adjustment can be made by using four layers of a piece of newspaper. The thickness of the paper is equivalent to about .020″, which is the approximate gap setting for most distributors. Of course, at the earliest opportunity, a precise point adjustment should be made.

If the procedure outlined under "Primary Ignition Checkout" does not uncover the trouble then it will be necessary to continue the tests into the secondary ignition circuit.

Secondary Ignition Checkout

First of all, remove the wire from one of the spark plugs, turn on the ignition and operate the starter. While the engine is cranking, hold the terminal of the spark plug wire about ¼″ away from the engine or spark plug base. If the spark is strong and jumps the gap, the trouble is confined to either the spark plugs or lack of fuel. Before going any further, wipe the outside of the plugs to remove any dirt or dampness which would create an easy path for the current to flow, then try to start the engine again. If it still fails to start, remove one of the spark plugs and if it is wet around the base, it indicates that the fuel system is okay, so it naturally follows that the spark plugs are at fault. Remove all the plugs, clean them and set the gaps. An

emergency adjustment of spark plug gais can be made by folding a piece of newspaper into 6 or 7 layers. When changing the gap, always bend the side (ground) electrode and never the center one as there is danger of breaking the insulation.

Fuel System Checkout

If the spark plug that was removed showed no indication of dampness on its base, check the fuel system. A quick check can be made by simply removing the carburetor air cleaner and looking down into the carburetor. Manually open and close the throttle at the carburetor. This action will cause the accelerator pump to spray fuel mixture which you can see by looking down into the throat of the carburetor. If it does spray, the check the choke valve. If the engine is cold, the choke valve should be closed. If the choke will not close, the engine can be started by covering the carburetor throat with the palm of your hand while the engine is cranking, providing, of course, that fuel is reaching the carburetor.

If moving the throttle manually does not result in a spray of fuel mixture in the carburetor throat, then fuel is not reaching the carburetor.

Check the operation of the fuel pump by disconnecting the fuel lines from the pump to the carburetor. Crank the engine and if the pump is working, fuel will pulsate out of the line. If not, either the pump isn't working or the line from the tank to the pump is clogged. Before blaming the pump, however, disconnect the line at the inlet side of the pump which leads to the tank and, while a companion listens at the tank, blow through the line. If a gurgling sound is heard back in the tank, the line is open and the trouble is in the pump. Remove the sediment bowl, if so equipped and clean the screen, then replace the bowl and screen, being sure that you have an air-tight fit. If the pump still refuses to function, it should be removed and repaired.

The foregoing discussion will, in most cases, uncover the cause of why an engine won't start. However, if further diagnosis is necessary, the following list will undoubtedly provide the answer.

VAPOR LOCK

The term vapor lock means that the flow of fuel to the mixing chamber in the carburetor has been stopped (locked) by the formation of vaporized fuel pockets or bubbles caused by overheating the fuel by hot fuel pump, hot fuel lines or hot carburetor.

The more volatile the fuel the greater the tendency for it to vapor lock. Vapor lock is encouraged by high atmospheric temperature, hard driving, defective engine cooling and high altitude.

A mild case of vapor lock will cause missing and hard starting when engine is warm. Somewhat more severe vapor lock will stop the engine which cannot be started again until it has cooled off enough so that any vaporized fuel has condensed to a liquid.

SERVICE NOTE: Some cars equipped with air conditioning have a vapor bypass system. These cars have a special fuel filter which has a metering outlet in the top. Any vapor which forms is bled off and returned to the fuel tank through a separate line alongside the fuel supply line. This system greatly reduces the possibility of vapor lock. Therefore, if vapor lock is suspected examine the bypass valve to see if it is functioning.

PERCOLATION

Percolation means simply that gasoline in the carburetor bowl is boiling over into the intake manifold. This condition is most apt to occur immediately after a hot engine is shut off. Most carburetors have a provision for relieving the vapor pressure of overheated fuel in the carburetor bowl by means of ports. If, however, percolation should take place, the engine may be started by allowing it to cool slightly and then holding the throttle wide open while cranking to clear the intake manifold of excess fuel.

CARBURETOR ICING

The carburetor discharges liquid fuel into the air stream in the form of an atomized spray which evaporates readily. The heat required to evaporate the gasoline is drawn from the entering air, thereby lowering its temperature. The cooler air chills the interior of the carburetor and may cause the moisture in the air to condense into droplets.

Under certain conditions of atmospheric temperature and humidity, the liberated moisture actually collects and freezes on the chilled carburetor surfaces, especially on the throttle plate and surrounding throttle body. When the throttle is almost completely closed for idling, this ice tends to bridge the gap between the throttle plate and throttle body, thereby cutting off the air supply and causing the engine to stall. Opening the throttle for restarting breaks the ice bridge but does not eliminate the possibility of further stalling until the engine and carburetor has warmed up.

For carburetor icing to occur, the outside air must be cool enough so that the refrigerating effect of fuel evaporation in the carburetor will lower the temperatures of the throttle plate and body below both the dew point of moist air and the freezing point of water. The air must also contain sufficient moisture for appreciable condensation of water to occur when it is chilled in the carburetor.

Generally speaking, carburetor icing occurs when winter grade gasoline (more volatile than summer grade) is used and when the atmospheric temperature ranges from 30° to 50° F. at relative humidities in excess of 65%.

Carburetor icing problems can be reduced by the use of anti-icing additives, such as alcohols, in the fuel. Some fuel refiners use anti-stalling additives in their gasolines which have proved effective in combating carburetor icing.

Another form of carburetor icing has been observed in some engines during high-speed driving on cool, moist days. When certain cars are driven steadily at 60 to 80 mph, the large quantities of cool air passing through the carburetor may result in gradual ice formation within the carburetor's venturi. Since this ice restricts the venturi passage, the resultant increased vacuum in the venturi tends to increase the rate of fuel flow. The fuel-air mixture thus becomes excessively rich, causing loss of power and high fuel consumption.

SPARK KNOCK, PING, DETONATION

All three expressions mean the same thing. It is a sharp metallic knock caused by vibration of the cylinder head and block. The vibration is due to split-second high-pressure waves resulting from almost instantaneous abnormal combustion instead of the slower normal combustion.

The ping may be mild or loud. A mild ping does no harm but a severe ping will reduce power. A very severe ping may shatter spark plugs, break valves or crack pistons.

Pinging is most likely to occur on open throttle at low or moderate engine speed. Pinging is encouraged by:

1. Overheated engine.
2. Low octane fuel.
3. Too high compression.
4. Spark advanced too far.
5. Hot mixture due to hot engine or hot weather.
6. Heavy carbon deposit which increases the compression pressure.

If an engine pings objectionably because of the use of fuel with too low an octane rating, the ignition timing can be retarded (set back) slightly to reduce the tendence to ping. Be sure, though, that the cooling system is in good condition and that the carburetor mixture has been properly set. Hot particles of carbon in the combustion chamber will also contribute to pinging. Such particles would be removed during a valve job.

PRE-IGNITION

Pre-ignition means that the mixture is set on fire before the spark occurs, being ignited by a red hot spot in the combustion chamber such as an incandescent particle of carbon; a thin piece of protruding metal; an overheated spark plug, or a bright red hot exhaust valve. The result is reduction of power and overheating accompanied by pinging. The bright red hot exhaust valve may be due to a leak, to lack of tappet clearance, to valve sticking, or a weak or broken spring.

Pre-ignition may not be noticed if not severe. Severe pre-ignition results in severe pinging. The most common cause of pre-ignition is a badly overheated engine.

When the engine won't stop when the ignition is shut off, the cause is often due to red hot carbon particles resting on heavy carbon deposit in a very hot engine.

AFTER-BURNING

A subdued put-putting at the exhaust tail pipe may be due to leaky exhaust valves which permit the mixture to finish combusion in the muffler. If exhaust pipe or muffler is red hot, better let it cool, as there is some danger. of setting the car on fire. Be sure the carburetor mixture is properly adjusted.

ENGINE CONTINUES TO RUN AFTER IGNITION IS TURNED OFF

This condition, known as "dieseling," "run on," or "after running," is caused by improper idle speed and/or high temperature. Idle speed and engine temperature are affected by:

Carburetor Adjustment: High idle speed will increase the tendency to diesel because of the inertia of the engine crankshaft and flywheel. Too low an idle speed, particularly with a lean mixture, will result in an increase in engine temperature, especially if the engine is allowed to idle for long periods of time.

Ignition Timing: Because advanced ignition timing causes a corresponding increase in idle speed and retarded timing reduces idle speed, ignition timing influences the tendency to diesel in the same manner as Carburetor Adjustment.

Fuel Mixture: Enriching the idle fuel mixture decreases the tendency to diesel by causing the engine to run cooler.

Fuel Content: High octane fuels tend to reduce dieseling. Increased fuel content of lead alkyl increases the tendency to diesel. Phosphates and nickel fuel additives help prevent dieseling.

Spark Plugs: Plugs of too high a heat range for the engine in question can cause dieseling.

Throttle Plates: If the throttle plates are not properly aligned in the carburetor bore, a resulting leanness in fuel mixture occurs, contributing to dieseling.

Electrical System: Normally, during dieseling, ignition is self-supplied by a "hot spot," self-igniting fuel, etc. However, there is a possibility of the vehicle's electrical system supplying the necessary ignition. When the ignition switch is turned off, a small amount of current can flow from the generator into the primary of the ignition coil through the generator tell-tale light. This is particularly true when the warning light bulb has been changed for one of increased wattage.

NOTE: "Run on" is more prevalent in an engine when the ignition is turned off before the engine is allowed to return to idle. Therefore, it can be reduced by letting the engine return to idle before shutting off the ignition. "Run on" incidence can be reduced on automatic transmittion units by turning off the engine when in gear.

A certain amount of "run on" can be expected from any gasoline engine regardless of make, size or configuration. (Diesel engines operate on this principle.) However, if the above suggestions are correctly employed, "run on" will be reduced to an unnoticeable level.

ENGINE NOISE TESTS

Noises emanating from a running engine are warning signs that should be attended to. For example, a slightly worn rod bearing may begin to knock because the oil level is too low or the oil is no longer usable. Continued operation of the engine, in this condition, may cause scoring of the crankshaft which would only run the repair expense higher. Pay attention to all of the engine noises that are listed below. They can cause expensive repairs if allowed to continue.

Loose Main Bearing

A loose main bearing is indicated by a powerful but dull thud or knock when the engine is pulling. If all main bearings are loose a noticeable clatter will be audible.

The thud occurs regularly every other revolution. The knock can be confirmed by shorting spark plugs on cylinders adjacent to the bearing. Knock will disappear or be less when plugs are shorted. This test should be made at a fast idle equivalent to 15 mph in high gear. If the bearing is not loose enough to produce the knock by itself, the bearing may knock if oil is too thin or if there is no oil at the bearing.

Loose Flywheel

A thud or click which is usually irregular. To test, idle the engine at about 20 mph and shut off the ignition. If thud is heard, the flywheel may be loose.

Loose Rod Bearing

A metallic knock which is usually loudest at about 30 mph with throttle closed. Knock can be reduced or even eliminated by shorting spark plug. If the bearing is not loose enough to produce the knock by itself, the bearing may knock if oil is too thin or if there is no oil at the bearing.

Piston Pin

Piston pin, piston and connecting rod noises are difficult to tell apart.

A loose piston pin causes a sharp double knock which is usually heard when engine is idling. The severity of knock should increase when spark plug to this cylinder is short-circuited. However, on some engines the knock becomes more noticeable at 25 to 35 mph on the road.

Hydraulic Lifters

The malfunctioning of a hydraulic valve lifter is almost always accompanied by a clicking or tapping noise. Hydraulic lifter noise may be expected when the engine is cold but if lifters are functioning properly the noise should disappear when the engine warms up.

If all or nearly all lifters are noisy, they may be stuck because of dirty or gummy oil.

If all lifters are noisy, oil pressure to them may be inadequate. Foaming oil may also cause this trouble. If oil foams there will be bubbles on the oil level dipstick. Foaming may be caused by water in the oil or by too high an oil level or by a very low oil level.

If the hydraulic lifters require an initial adjustment, they will be noisy if this adjustment is incorrect.

If one lifter is noisy the cause may be:

1. Plunger too tight in lifter body.
2. Weak or broken plunger spring.
3. Ball valve leaks.
4. Plunger worn.
5. Lock ring (if any) improperly installed or missing.
6. Lack of oil pressure to this plunger.

If ball valve leaks, clean plunger in special solvent such as acetone and reinstall. Too often, plungers are condemned as faulty when all they need is a thorough cleaning.

Gum and dirty oil are the most common causes of hydraulic valve lifter trouble. Engine oil must be free of dirt. Select a standard brand of engine oil and use no other. Mixing up one standard brand with another may cause gummy oil and sticking plungers. Do not use any special oils unless recommended by the car manufacturer and change oil filter or element at recommended intervals.

Loose Engine Mountings

Loose engine mountings are indicated by an occasional thud with the car in operation. The thud will most likely be noticed at the moment the throttle is opened or closed.

Excessive Crankshaft End Play

Excessive crankshaft end play is indicated by a rather sharp rap which occurs at idling speed but may also be heard at higher speeds. The noise should disappear when the clutch is disengaged.

Fuel Pump Noise

Diagnosis of fuel pumps suspected as noisy requires that some form of sounding device be used. Judgment by ear alone is not sufficient, otherwise a fuel pump may be needlessly replaced in attempting to correct noise contributed by some other component. Use of a stethoscope, a long screwdriver, or a sounding rod is recommended to locate the area or component causing the noise. The sounding rod can easily be made from a length of copper tubing ¼ to ⅜ inch in diameter.

With the engine running, hold the rod against the engine in the area of the noise. Listen at the other end of the rod. The noise will sound amplified and distinctive as you move the rod closer to the area of the noise.

If the noise has been isolated to the fuel pump, remove the pump and run the engine with the fuel remaining in the carburetor bowl. If the noise level does not change, the source of the noise is elsewhere and the original fuel pump should be reinstalled. On models using a fuel pump push rod, check for excessive wear and/or galling of the push rod.

ENGINE

• PROBLEM — ENGINE WILL NOT START

Possible Cause	*Correction*
1. Weak battery.	1. Test battery specific gravity. Recharge or replace as necessary.
2. Corroded or loose battery connections.	2. Clean and tighten battery connections. Apply a coat of petroleum jelly to terminals.
3. Faulty starter.	3. Repair starter motor.
4. Moisture on ignition wires and distributor cap.	4. Wipe wires and cap clean and dry.
5. Faulty ignition cables.	5. Replace any cracked or shorted cables.
6. Open or shorted primary ignition circuit.	6. Trace primary ignition circuit and repair as necessary.
7. Malfunctioning ignition points or condenser or electronic component.	7. Replace ignition points & condenser as necessary.
8. Faulty coil.	8. Test and replace if necessary.
9. Incorrect spark plug gap.	9. Set gap correctly.
10. Incorrect ignition timing.	10. Reset timing.
11. Dirt or water in fuel line or carburetor.	11. Clean lines and carburetor. Replace filter.
12. Carburetor flooded.	12. Adjust float level—check seats.
13. Incorrect carburetor float setting.	13. Adjust float level—check seats.
14. Faulty fuel pump.	14. Install new fuel pump.
15. Carburetor percolating. No fuel in the carburetor.	15. Measure float level. Adjust bowl vent. Inspect operation of manifold heat control valve.

• PROBLEM — ENGINE STALLS

Possible Cause	*Correction*
1. Idle speed set too low.	1. Adjust carburetor.
2. Incorrect choke adjustment.	2. Adjust choke.
3. Idle mixture too lean or too rich.	3. Adjust carburetor.
4. Incorrect carburetor float setting.	4. Adjust float setting.

5. Leak in intake manifold.	5. Inspect intake manifold gasket and replace if necessary.
6. Worn or burned distributor rotor.	6. Install new rotor.
7. Incorrect ignition wiring.	7. Install correct wiring.
8. Faulty coil.	8. Test and replace if necessary.
9. Incorrect tappet lash.	9. Adjust to specifications.

• PROBLEM — ENGINE LOSS OF POWER

Possible Cause   *Correction*

1. Incorrect ignition timing.	1. Reset timing.
2. Worn or burned distributor rotor.	2. Install new rotor.
3. Worn distributor shaft.	3. Remove and repair distributor.
4. Dirty or incorrectly gapped spark plugs.	4. Clean plugs and set gap.
5. Dirt or water in fuel line, carburetor or filter.	5. Clean lines, carburetor and replace filter.
6. Incorrect carburetor float setting.	6. Adjust float level.
7. Faulty fuel pump.	7. Install new pump.
8. Incorrect valve timing.	8. Check and correct valve timing.
9. Blown cylinder head gasket.	9. Install new head gasket.
10. Low compression.	10. Test compression of each cylinder.
11. Burned, warped or pitted valves.	11. Install new valves.
12. Plugged or restricted exhaust system.	12. Install new parts as necessary.
13. Faulty ignition cables.	13. Replace any cracked or shorted cables.
14. Faulty coil.	14. Test and replace as necessary.

• PROBLEM — ENGINE MISSES ON ACCELERATION

Possible Cause   *Correction*

1. Dirty, or gap too wide in spark plugs.	1. Clean spark plugs and set gap.
2. Incorrect ignition timing.	2. Reset timing.
3. Dirt in carburetor.	3. Clean carburetor and replace filter.
4. Acceleration pump in carburetor.	4. Install new pump.
5. Burned, warped or pitted valves.	5. Install new valves.
6. Faulty coil.	6. Test and replace if necessary.

TDG 14

• PROBLEM — ENGINE MISSES AT HIGH SPEED

Possible Cause	*Correction*
1. Dirty or gap set too wide in spark plug.	1. Clean spark plugs and set gap.
2. Worn distributor shaft.	2. Remove and repair distributor.
3. Worn or burned distributor rotor.	3. Install new rotor.
4. Faulty coil.	4. Test and replace if necessary.
5. Incorrect ignition timing.	5. Reset timing.
6. Dirty jets in carburetor.	6. Clean carburetor, replace filter.
7. Dirt or water in fuel line, carburetor or filter.	7. Clean lines, carburetor and replace filter.

• PROBLEM — NOISY VALVES

Possible Cause	*Correction*
1. High or low oil level in crankcase.	1. Check for correct oil level.
2. Thin or diluted oil.	2. Change oil.
3. Low oil pressure.	3. Check engine oil level.
4. Dirt in valve lifters.	4. Clean lifters.
5. Bent push rods.	5. Install new push rods.
6. Worn rocker arms.	6. Inspect oil supply to rockers.
7. Worn tappets.	7. Install new tappets.
8. Worn valve guides.	8. Ream and install new valves with O/S stems.
9. Excessive run-out of valve seats or valves faces.	9. Grind valve seats and valves.
10. Incorrect tappet lash.	10. Adjust to specifications.

• PROBLEM — CONNECTING ROD NOISE

Possible Cause	*Correction*
1. Insufficient oil supply.	1. Check engine oil level.
2. Low oil pressure.	2. Check engine oil level. Inspect oil pump relief valve and spring.
3. Thin or diluted oil.	3. Change oil to correct viscosity.
4. Excessive bearing clearance.	4. Measure bearings for correct clearance.
5. Connecting rod journals out-of-round.	5. Replace crankshaft or regrind journals.
6. Misaligned (bent) connecting rods.	6. Replace bent connecting rods.

• PROBLEM — MAIN BEARING NOISE

Possible Cause	*Correction*
1. Insufficient oil supply.	1. Check engine oil level.
2. Low oil pressure.	2. Check engine oil level. Inspect oil pump relief valve and spring.
3. Thin or diluted oil.	3. Change oil to correct viscosity.
4. Excessive bearing clearance.	4. Measure bearings for correct clearances.
5. Excessive end play.	5. Check thrust bearing for wear on flanges.
6. Crankshaft journal out-of-round worn.	6. Replace crankshaft or regrind journals.
7. Loose flywheel or torque converter.	7. Tighten to correct torque.

• PROBLEM — OIL PUMPING AT RINGS

Possible Cause	*Correction*
1. Worn, scuffed, or broken rings.	1. Hone cylinder bores and install new rings.
2. Carbon in oil ring slot.	2. Install new rings.
3. Rings fitted too tight in grooves.	3. Remove the rings. Check grooves. If groove is not proper width, replace piston.

• PROBLEM — OIL PRESSURE DROP

Possible Cause	*Correction*
1. Low oil level.	1. Check engine oil level.
2. Faulty oil pressure sending unit.	2. Install new sending unit.
3. Clogged oil filter.	3. Install new oil filter.
4. Worn parts in oil pump.	4. Replace worn parts or pump.
5. Thin or diluted oil.	5. Change oil to correct viscosity.
6. Excessive bearing clearance.	6. Measure bearings for correct clearance.
7. Oil pump relief valve stuck.	7. Remove valve and inspect, clean, and reinstall.
8. Oil pump suction tube loose, bent or cracked.	8. Remove oil pan and install new tube if necessary.

• PROBLEM — NO OIL PRESSURE

Possible Cause   *Correction*

1. Low oil level.
2. Oil pressure gauge or sending unit inaccurate.
3. Oil pump malfunction.
4. Oil pressure relief valve sticking.

5. Oil passages on pressure side of pump obstructed.
6. Oil pickup screen or tube obstructed.

1. Add oil to correct level.

2. Replace defective unit.
3. Repair oil pump.
4. Remove and inspect oil pressure relief valve assembly.
5. Inspect oil passages for obstructions.
6. Inspect oil pickup for obstructions.

• PROBLEM — LOW OIL PRESSURE

Possible Cause   *Correction*

1. Low oil level.
2. Oil excessively thin due to dilution, poor quality, or improper grade.
3. Oil pressure relief spring weak or sticking.
4. Oil pickup tube and screen assembly has restriction or air leak.

5. Excessive oil pump clearance.
6. Excessive main, rod, or camshaft bearing clearance.

1. Add oil to correct level.
2. Drain and refill crankcase with recommended oil.

3. Remove and inspect oil pressure relief valve assembly.
4. Remove and inspect oil inlet tube and screen assembly (Fill pickup with lacquer thinner to find leaks.)
5. Check clearances.
6. Measure bearing clearances, repair as necessary.

• PROBLEM — HIGH OIL PRESSURE

Possible Cause   *Correction*

1. Improper grade oil.

2. Oil pressure gauge or sending unit inaccurate.
3. Oil pressure relief valve sticking closed.

1. Drain and refill crankcase with correct grade oil.
2. Replace defective unit.

3. Remove and inspect oil pressure relieve valve assembly.

• PROBLEM — EXTERNAL OIL LEAK

Possible Cause	*Correction*
1. Fuel pump gasket broken or improperly seated.	1. Replace gasket.
2. Cylinder head cover gasket broken or improperly seated.	2. Replace gasket; check cylinder head cover gasket flange and cylinder head gasket surface for distortion.
3. Oil filter gasket broken or improperly seated.	3. Replace oil filter.
4. Oil pan side gasket broken or improperly seated.	4. Replace gasket; check oil pan gasket flange for distortion.
5. Oil pan front oil seal broken or improperly seated.	5. Replace seal; check timing chain cover and oil pan seal flange for distortion.
6. Oil pan rear oil seal broken or improperly seated.	6. Replace seal; check oil pan rear oil seal flange; check rear main bearing cap for cracks, plugged oil return channels, or distortion in seal groove.
7. Timing chain cover oil seal broken or improperly seated.	7. Replace seal.
8. Oil pan drain plug loose or has stripped threads.	8. Repair as necessary and tighten.
9. Rear oil gallery plug loose.	9. Use appropriate sealant on gallery plug and tighten.
10. Rear camshaft plug loose or improperly seated.	10. Seat camshaft plug or replace and seal, as necessary.

• PROBLEM — EXCESSIVE OIL CONSUMPTION

Possible Cause	*Correction*
1. Oil level too high.	1. Lower oil level to specifications.
2. Oil too thin.	2. Replace with specified oil.
3. Valve stem oil seals are damaged, missing, or incorrect type.	3. Replace valve stem oil seals.
4. Valve stems or valve guides worn.	4. Check stem-to-guide clearance and repair as necessary.
5. Piston rings broken, missing.	5. Replace missing or broken rings.
6. Piston rings incorrect size.	6. Check ring gap, repair as necessary.

7. Piston rings sticking or excessively loose in grooves.

8. Compression rings installed upside down.

9. Cylinder walls worn, scored, or glazed.

10. Piston rings gaps not properly staggered.

11. Excessive main or connecting rod bearing clearance.

7. Check ring side clearance, repair as necessary.

8. Repair as necessary.

9. Repair as necessary.

10. Repair as necessary.

11. Check bearing clearance, repair as necessary.

OIL PRESSURE INDICATOR

- **PROBLEM — LIGHT NOT LIT, IGNITION ON AND ENGINE NOT RUNNING.**

Possible Cause

Correction

1. Bulb burned out.
2. Open in light circuit.
3. Defective oil pressure switch.

1. Replace bulb.
2. Locate and correct open.
3. Replace oil pressure switch.

- **PROBLEM — LIGHT ON, ENGINE RUNNING ABOVE IDLE SPEED.**

Possible Cause

Correction

1. Grounded wiring between light and switch.
2. Defective oil pressure switch.
3. Low oil pressure.

1. Locate and repair ground.
2. Replace oil pressure switch.
3. Locate cause of low oil pressure and correct.

IGNITION, STARTER & FUEL

- **PROBLEM — NOTHING HAPPENS WHEN START ATTEMPT IS MADE**

Possible Cause

Correction

1. Undercharged or defective battery.
2. Loose battery cables.

1. Check condition of battery and recharge or replace as required.
2. Clean and tighten cable connections.

3. Burned fusible link in starting circuit.

3. Check for burned fusible link. Correct wiring problem.

4. Incorrectly positioned or defective neutral start switch.

4. Check neutral start switch adjustment. If O.K., replace switch.

5. Loose or defective wiring between neutral start switch and ignition switch.

5. Check for loose connections and opens between battery, horn relay, ignition switch, and solenoid "S" terminal. Check battery ground cable. Replace or repair defective item.

6. Defective starter motor.

6. Repair or replace starter motor.

7. Defective starter interlock system.

7. Use emergency button under hood. If car starts, repair circuit in interlock system. If car does not start, check and repair starter circuit.

• PROBLEM — SOLENOID SWITCH CLICKS BUT STARTER DOES NOT CRANK

Possible Cause

Correction

1. Undercharged or defective battery.

1. Test battery. Recharge or replace battery.

2. Loose battery cables.

2. Check and tighten battery connections.

3. Loose or defective wiring at starter.

3. Tighten connections or repair wiring as required.

4. Defective solenoid.

4. Replace solenoid.

5. "Hot stall" condition.

5. Check engine cooling system.

6. Excessive engine rotational torque caused by mechanical problem within engine.

6. Check engine torque for excessive friction.

7. Defective starter motor.

7. Repair or replace starter motor.

• PROBLEM — SLOW CRANKING

Possible Cause

Correction

1. Vehicle is overheating.

1. Check engine cooling system and repair as required.

2. Undercharged or defective battery.

2. Recharge or replace battery.

3. Loose or defective wiring between battery and engine block.	3. Repair or replace wiring.
4. Loose or defective wiring between battery and solenoid "Bat" terminal.	4. Repair or replace wiring.
5. Defective starter motor.	5. Repair or replace starter.

- **PROBLEM — STARTER SPINS AND/OR MAKES LOUD GRINDING NOISE BUT DOES NOT TURN ENGINE**

Possible Cause	*Correction*
1. Defective starter motor.	1. Repair or replace starter motor.
2. Defective ring gear.	2. Replace ring gear.

- **PROBLEM — STARTER KEEPS RUNNING AFTER IGNITION SWITCH IS RELEASED—FROM "START" TO "RUN" POSITION**

Possible Cause	*Correction*
1. Defective ignition switch.	1. Replace ignition switch.
2. Defective solenoid.	2. Replace solenoid.

- **PROBLEM — STARTER ENGAGES ("CLUNKS") BUT ENGINE DOES NOT CRANK**

Possible Cause	*Correction*
1. Open circuit in solenoid armature or field coils.	1. Repair or replace solenoid or starter motor.
2. Short or ground in field coil or armature.	2. Repair or replace starter motor.

- **PROBLEM — HARD STARTING (ENGINE CRANKS NORMALLY)**

Possible Cause	*Correction*
1. Binding linkage choke valve or choke piston.	1. Repair as necessary.
2. Restricted choke vacuum and hot air passages.	2. Clean passages.
3. Improper fuel level.	3. Adjust float level.
4. Dirty, worn or faulty needle valve and seat.	4. Repair as necessary.

5. Float sticking.
6. Exhaust manifold heat valve stuck.
7. Faulty fuel pump.
8. Incorrect choke cover adjustment.
9. Inadequate unloader adjustment.
10. Faulty ignition coil.
11. Improper spark plug gap.
12. Incorrect initial timing.
13. Incorrect valve timing.

5. Repair as necessary.
6. Repair as necessary.
7. Replace fuel pump.
8. Adjust choke cover.
9. Adjust unloader.
10. Test and replace as necessary.
11. Adjust gap.
12. Adjust timing.
13. Check valve timing; repair as necessary.

• PROBLEM — ROUGH IDLE OR STALLING

Possible Cause

Correction

1. Incorrect curb or fast idle speed.
2. Incorrect initial timing.
3. Improper idle mixture adjustment.
4. Damaged tip on idle mixture screw(s).
5. Improper fast idle cam adjustment.
6. Faulty PCV valve air flow.

7. Exhaust manifold heat valve inoperative.
8. Choke binding.

9. Improper choke setting.
10. Vacuum leak.

11. Improper fuel level.
12. Faulty distributor rotor or cap.
13. Leaking engine valves.

14. Incorrect ignition wiring.

15. Faulty coil.
16. Clogged air bleed or idle passages.
17. Restricted air cleaner.
18. Faulty EGR valve operation if equipped.

1. Adjust curb or fast idle speed.
2. Adjust timing to specifications.
3. Adjust idle mixture.
4. Replace mixture screw(s).

5. Adjust fast idle.
6. Test PCV valve and replace as necessary.
7. Lubricate or replace heat valve as necessary.
8. Locate and eliminate binding condition.
9. Adjust choke.
10. Check manifold vacuum and repair as necessary.
11. Adjust fuel level.
12. Replace rotor or cap.
13. Check cylinder leakdown rate or compression and repair as necessary.
14. Check wiring and correct as necessary.
15. Test coil and replace as necessary.
16. Clean passages.
17. Clean or replace air cleaner.
18. Test EGR system and replace as necessary if equipped.

● PROBLEM — FAULTY LOW-SPEED OPERATION

Possible Cause	Correction
1. Clogged idle transfer slots.	1. Clean transfer slots.
2. Restricted idle air bleeds and passages.	2. Clean air bleeds and passages.
3. Restricted air cleaner.	3. Clean or replace air cleaner.
4. Improper fuel level.	4. Adjust fuel level.
5. Faulty spark plugs.	5. Clean or replace spark plugs.
6. Dirty, corroded, or loose secondary circuit connections.	6. Clean or tighten secondary circuit connections.
7. Faulty ignition cable.	7. Replace ignition cable.
8. Faulty distributor cap.	8. Replace cap.

● PROBLEM — FAULY ACCELERATION

Possible Cause	Correction
1. Improper pump stroke.	1. Adjust pump stroke.
2. Incorrect ignition timing.	2. Adjust timing.
3. Inoperative pump discharge check ball or needle.	3. Clean or replace as necessary.
4. Worn or damaged pump diaphragm or piston.	4. Replace diaphragm or piston.
5. Leaking main body cover gasket.	5. Replace gasket.
6. Engine cold and choke too lean.	6. Adjust choke.
7. Faulty spark plug(s).	7. Clean or replace spark plug(s).
8. Leaking engine valves.	8. Check cylinder leakdown rate or compression, repair as necessary.
9. Faulty coil.	9. Test coil and replace as necessary.

● PROBLEM — FAULTY HIGH-SPEED OPERATION

Possible Cause	Correction
1. Incorrect ignition timing.	1. Adjust timing.
2. Faulty distributor centrifugal advance.	2. Check centrifugal advance and repair as necessary.
3. Faulty distributor vacuum advance.	3. Check vacuum advance and repair as necessary.
4. Low fuel pump volume.	4. Replace fuel pump.
5. Improper spark plug gap.	5. Adjust gap.
6. Faulty choke operation.	6. Adjust choke.
7. Partially restricted exhaust manifold.	7. Eliminate restriction.

8. Clogged vacuum passages.	8. Clean passages.
9. Improper size or obstructed main jets.	9. Clean or replace as necessary.
10. Restricted air cleaner.	10. Clean or replace as necessary.
11. Faulty distributor rotor or cap.	11. Replace rotor or cap.
12. Worn distributor shaft.	12. Replace shaft.
13. Faulty coil.	13. Test coil and replace as necessary.
14. Leaking engine valve(s).	14. Check cylinder leak down or compression and repair as necesary.
15. Faulty valve spring(s).	15. Inspect and test valve spring tension and replace as neceaary.
16. Incorrect valve timing.	16. Check valve timing and repair as necessary.
17. Intake manifold restricted.	17. Pass chain through passages.

• PROBLEM — MISFIRE AT ALL SPEEDS

Possible Cause	*Correction*
1. Faulty spark plug(s).	1. Clean or replace spark plug(s).
2. Faulty spark plug cable(s).	2. Replace as necessary.
3. Faulty distributor cap or rotor.	3. Replace cap or rotor.
4. Faulty coil.	4. Test coil and replace as necessary.
5. Primary circuit shorted or open intermittently.	5. Trace primary circuit and repair as necessary.
6. Leaking engine valve(s).	6. Check cylinder leakdown rate or compression and repair as necessary.
7. Faulty hydraulic tappet(s).	7. Clean or replace tappet(s).
8. Faulty valve spring(s).	8. Inspect and test valve spring tension, repair as necessary.
9. Worn lobes on camshaft.	9. Replace camshaft.
10. Vacuum leak.	10. Check manifold vacuum and repair as necessary.
11. Improper carburetor settings.	11. Adjust carburetor.
12. Fuel pump volume or pressure	12. Replace fuel pump.
13. Blown cylinder head gasket.	13. Replace gasket.
14. Intake or exhaust manifold passage(s) restricted.	14. Pass chain through passages.

• PROBLEM — POWER NOT UP TO NORMAL

Possible Cause	*Correction*
1. Incorrect ignition timing.	1. Adjust timing.

2. Faulty distributor rotor.
3. Worn distributor shaft.
4. Incorrect spark plug gap.
5. Faulty fuel pump.
6. Incorrect valve timing.

7. Faulty coil.
8. Faulty ignition cables.

9. Leaking engine valves.

10. Blown cylinder head gasket.
11. Leaking piston rings.

2. Replace rotor.
3. Replace shaft.
4. Adjust gap.
5. Replace fuel pump.
6. Check valve timing and repair as necessary.

7. Test coil and replace as necessary.
8. Test cables and replace as necessary.

9. Check cylinder leakdown rate or compression and repair as necessary.

10. Replace gasket.
11. Check compression and repair as necessary.

• PROBLEM — INTAKE BACKFIRE

Possible Cause

1. Improper ignition timing.
2. Faulty accelerator pump discharge.
3. Improper choke operation.
4. Lean fuel mixture.

Correction

1. Adjust timing.
2. Repair as necessary.

3. Repair as necessary.
4. Check float level or manifold vacuum for vacuum leak.

• PROBLEM — EXHAUST BACKFIRE

Possible Cause

1. Vacuum leak.

2. Faulty A.I.R. diverter valve.

3. Faulty choke operation.
4. Exhaust leak.

Correction

1. Check manifold vacuum and repair as necessary.

2. Test diverter valve and replace as necessary.

3. Repair as necessary.
4. Locate and eliminate leak.

• PROBLEM — PING OR SPARK KNOCK

Possible Cause

1. Incorrect ignition timing.
2. Distributor centrifugal or vacuum advance malfunction.

Correction

1. Adjust timing.
2. Check advance and repair as necessary.

3. Excessive combustion chamber deposits.
4. Carburetor set too lean.
5. Vacuum leak.

6. Excessively high compression.

7. Fuel octane rating excessively low.
8. Heat riser stuck in heat on position.

3. Use combustion chamber cleaner.

4. Adjust carburetor.
5. Check manifold vacuum and repair as necessary.
6. Check compression and repair as necessary.
7. Try alternate fuel source.

8. Free-up or replace heat riser.

- **PROBLEM — SURGING (CRUISING SPEEDS TO TOP SPEEDS)**

Possible Cause

Correction

1. Low fuel level.
2. Low fuel pump pressure or volume.
3. Improper PCV valve air flow.

4. Vacuum leak.

5. Dirt in carburetor.
6. Undersize main jets.
7. Clogged fuel filter screen.
8. Restricted air cleaner.

1. Adjust fuel level.

2. Replace fuel pump.
3. Test PCV valve and replace as necessary.
4. Check manifold vacuum and repair as necessary.
5. Clean carburetor, replace filter.
6. Replace main jet(s).
7. Replace fuel filter.
8. Clean or replace air cleaner.

CHARGING SYSTEM

- **PROBLEM — ALTERNATOR FAILS TO CHARGE (No Output or Low Output)**

Possible Cause

Correction

1. Alternator drive belt loose.
2. Regulator base improperly grounded.
3. Worn brushes and/or slip rings.

4. Sticking brushes.

1. Adjust drive belt to specifications.
2. Connect regulator to a good ground.
3. Install new brushes and/or slip rings.
4. Clean slip rings and brush holders. Install new brushes if necessary.

5. Open field circuit.	5. Test all the field circuit connections, and correct as required.
6. Open charging circuit.	6. Inspect all connections in charging circuit, and correct as required.
7. Open circuit in stator windings.	7. Remove alternator and disassemble. Test stator windings. Install new stator if necessary.
8. Open rectifiers.	8. Remove alternator and disassemble. Test the rectifiers. Install new rectifier assemblies if necessary.

• PROBLEM — LOW, UNSTEADY CHARGING RATE

Possible Cause	*Correction*
1. High resistance in body to engine ground lead.	1. Tighten ground lead connections. Install new ground lead if necessary.
2. Alternator drive belt loose.	2. Adjust alternator drive belt.
3. High resistance at battery terminals.	3. Clean and tighten battery terminals.
4. High resistance in charging circuit.	4. Test charging circuit resistance. Correct as required.
5. Open stator winding.	5. Remove and disassemble alternator. Test stator windings. Install new stator if necessary.

• PROBLEM — LOW OUTPUT AND A LOW BATTERY

Possible Cause	*Correction*
1. High resistance in charging circuit.	1. Test charging circuit resistance and correct as required.
2. Shorted rectifier. Open rectifier.	2. Perform current output test. Test the rectifiers and install new rectifier heat sink assembly as required. Remove and disassemble the alternator.
3. Grounded stator windings.	3. Remove and disassemble alternator. Test stator windings. Install new stator if necessary.
4. Faulty voltage regulator.	4. Test voltage regulator. Replace as necessary.

- **PROBLEM — EXCESSIVE CHARGING RATE TO A FULLY CHARGED BATTERY**

Possible Cause	Correction
1. Faulty ignition switch.	1. Install new ignition switch.
2. Faulty voltage regulator.	2. Test voltage regulator. Replace as necessary.

- **PROBLEM — NOISY ALTERNATOR**

Possible Cause	Correction
1. Alternator mounting loose.	1. Properly install and tighten alternator mounting.
2. Worn or frayed drive belt.	2. Install a new drive belt and adjust to specifications.
3. Worn bearings.	3. Remove and disassemble alternator. Install new bearings as required.
4. Interference between rotor fan and stator leads.	4. Remove and disassemble alternator. Correct interference as required.
5. Rotor or rotor fan damaged.	5. Remove and disassemble alternator. Install new rotor.
6. Open or shorted rectifier.	6. Remove and disassemble alternator. Test rectifiers. Install new rectifier heat sink assembly as required.
7. Open or shorted winding in stator.	7. Remove and disassemble alternator. Test stator windings. Install new stator if necessary.

- **PROBLEM — EXCESSIVE AMMETER FLUCTUATION**

Possible Cause	Correction
1. High resistance in the alternator and voltage regulator circuit.	1. Clean and tighten all connections as necessary.

CHARGING SYSTEM INDICATOR

- **PROBLEM — LIGHT ON, IGNITION OFF.**

Possible Cause   *Correction*

1. Shorted positive diode.

1. Locate and replace shorted diode.

- **PROBLEM — LIGHT NOT ON, IGNITION ON AND ENGINE NOT RUNNING.**

Possible Cause   *Correction*

1. Bulb burned out.
2. Open in light circuit.
3. Open in field.

1. Replace bulb.
2. Locate and correct open.
3. Replace rotor.

- **PROBLEM — LIGHT ON, ENGINE RUNNING ABOVE IDLE SPEED.**

Possible Cause   *Correction*

1. No generator output.

2. Shortened negative diode.
3. Loose or broken generator belt.

1. Check and correct cause of no output.
2. Locate and replace shorted diode.
3. Tighten or replace and tighten generator belt.

COOLING SYSTEM

- **PROBLEM — HIGH TEMPERATURE INDICATION-OVERHEATING**

Possible Cause   *Correction*

1. Coolant level low.
2. Fan belt loose.
3. Radiator hose(s) collapsed.
4. Radiator blocked to airflow.
5. Faulty radiator cap.
6. Car overloaded.
7. Ignition timing incorrect.
8. Idle speed low.
9. Air trapped in cooling system.
10. Car in heavy traffic.

1. Replenish coolant level.
2. Adjust fan belt.
3. Replace hose(s).
4. Remove restriction.
5. Replace cap.
6. Reduce load.
7. Adjust ignition timing.
8. Adjust idle speed.
9. Purge air.
10. Operate at fast idle intermittently to cool engine.

11. Incorrect cooling system component(s) installed.	11. Install proper component(s).
12. Faulty thermostat.	12. Replace thermostat.
13. Water pump shaft broken or impeller loose.	13. Replace water pump.
14. Radiator tubes clogged.	14. Flush radiator.
15. Cooling system clogged.	15. Flush system.
16. Casting flash in cooling passages.	16. Repair or replace as necessary. Flash may be visible by removing cooling system components or removing core plugs.
17. Brakes dragging.	17. Repair brakes.
18. Excessive engine friction.	18. Repair engine.
19. Car working beyond cooling system.	19. Install heavy-duty cooling fan and/or radiator.
20. Antifreeze concentration over 68%.	20. Lower antifreeze content.
21. Low anti-freeze concentration.	21. Add anti-freeze to provide a minimum 50% concentration.

- **PROBLEM — LOW TEMPERATURE INDICATION—OVERCOOLING**

Possible Cause	*Correction*
1. Improper fan being used.	1. Install proper fan.
2. Improper radiator.	2. Install proper radiator.
3. Thermostat stuck open.	3. Replace thermostat.
4. Improper fan pulley (too small).	4. Install proper pulley.

- **PROBLEM — COOLANT LOSS—BOILOVER**

Possible Cause	*Correction*
Refer to Overheating Causes in addition to the following:	
1. Overfilled cooling system.	1. Reduce coolant level to proper specification.
2. Quick shutdown after hard (hot) run.	2. Allow engine to run at fast idle prior to shutdown.
3. Air in system resulting in occasional ''burping'' of coolant.	3. Purge system.
4. Insufficient antifreeze allowing coolant boiling point to be too low.	4. Add antifreeze to raise boiling point.

TDG 30

5. Antifreeze deteriorated because of age or contamination.	5. Replace coolant.
6. Leaks due to loose hose clamps, loose nuts, bolts, drain plugs, faulty hoses, or defective radiator.	6. Pressure test system to locate leak then repair as necessary.
7. Faulty head gasket.	7. Replace head gasket.
8. Cracked head, manifold, or block.	8. Replace as necessary.

● **PROBLEM — COOLANT ENTRY INTO CRANKCASE OR CYLINDER**

Possible Cause	*Correction*
1. Faulty head gasket.	1. Replace head gasket.
2. Crack in head, manifold, or block.	2. Replace as necessary.

● **PROBLEM — COOLANT RECOVERY SYSTEM INOPERATIVE**

Possible Cause	*Correction*
1. Coolant level low.	1. Replenish coolant.
2. Leak in system.	2. Pressure test to isolate leak and repair as necessary.
3. Pressure cap not tight or gasket missing or leaking.	3. Repair as necessary.
4. Pressure cap defective.	4. Replace cap.
5. Overflow tube clogged or leaking.	5. Repair as necessary.
6. Recovery bottle vent plugged.	6. Remove restriction.

● **PROBLEM — NOISE**

Possible Cause	*Correction*
1. Fan contacting shroud.	1. Reposition shroud and check engine mounts.
2. Loose water pump impeller.	2. Replace pump.
3. Dry fan belt.	3. Apply belt dressing or replace belt.
4. Loose fan belt.	4. Adjust fan belt.
5. Rough surface on drive pulley.	5. Replace pulley.
6. Water pump bearing worn.	6. Remove belt to isolate. Replace pump.

TDG 31

COOLANT TEMPERATURE INDICATOR

- **PROBLEM — "HOT" INDICATOR; LIGHT NOT LIT WHEN CRANKING ENGINE.**

Possible Cause	*Correction*
1. Bulb burned out.	1. Replace bulb.
2. Open in light circuit.	2. Locate and correct open.
3. Defective ignition switch.	3. Replace ignition switch.

- **PROBLEM — LIGHT ON, ENGINE RUNNING.**

Possible Cause	*Correction*
1. Wiring grounded between light and switch.	1. Locate and correct grounded wiring.
2. Defective temperature switch.	2. Replace temperature switch.
3. Defective ignition switch.	3. Replace ignition switch.
4. High coolant temperature.	4. Locate and correct cause of high coolant temperature.

- **PROBLEM — NO COOLANT FLOW THROUGH HEATER CORE**

Possible Cause	*Correction*
1. Plugged return pipe in water pump.	1. Remove obstruction.
2. Heater hose collapsed or plugged.	2. Remove obstruction or replace hose.
3. Plugged heater core.	3. Remove obstruction or replace core.
4. Plugged outlet in thermostat housing.	4. Remove flash or obstruction.
5. Heater bypass hole in cylinder head plugged.	5. Remove obstruction.

EXHAUST SYSTEM

- **PROBLEM — LEAKING EXHAUST GASES**

Possible Cause	*Correction*
1. Leaks at pipe joints.	1. Tighten U-bolt nuts at leaking joints.

2. Damaged or improperly installed seals or packing.

3. Loose exhaust pipe heat tube extension connections.

4. Burned or rusted out exhaust pipe heat tube extensions.

2. Replace seals or packing as necessary.

3. Replace seals or packing as required. Tighten stud nuts or bolts.

4. Replace heat tube extensions as required.

• PROBLEM — EXHAUST NOISES

Possible Cause

Correction

1. Leaks at manifold or pipe connections.

2. Burned or blown out muffler.
3. Burned or rusted out exhaust pipe.
4. Exhaust pipe leaking at manifold flange.
5. Exhaust manifold cracked or broken.
6. Leak between manifold and cylinder head.

1. Tighten clamps at leaking connections to specified torque. Replace gasket or packing as required.

2. Replace muffler assembly.
3. Replace exhaust pipe.
4. Tighten attaching bolt nuts.

5. Replace manifold.

6. Tighten manifold to cylinder head stud nuts or bolts.

• PROBLEM — LOSS OF ENGINE POWER AND/OR INTERNAL RATTLES IN MUFFLER

Possible Cause

Correction

1. Dislodged turning tubes and/or baffles in muffler.

1. Replace muffler.

• PROBLEM — LOSS OF ENGINE POWER

Possible Cause

Correction

1. Imploding (inner wall collapse) of exhaust pipe.

1. Replace exhaust pipe.

• PROBLEM — ENGINE HARD TO WARM UP OR WILL NOT RETURN TO NORMAL IDLE

Possible Cause

Correction

1. Heat control valve frozen in the open position.

1. Free up manifold heat control using a suitable manifold heat control solvent.

- **PROBLEM — MANIFOLD HEAT CONTROL VALVE NOISE**

Possible Cause	*Correction*
1. Thermostat broken.	1. Replace thermostat.
2. Broken, weak or missing anti-rattle spring.	2. Replace spring..

CLUTCH & SYNCHRO-MESH TRANSMISSION

- **PROBLEM — CLUTCH FAILS TO RELEASE, PEDAL PRESSED TO FLOOR-SHIFT LEVER DOES NOT MOVE FREELY IN AND OUT OF GEAR**

Possible Cause	*Correction*
1. Improper linkage adjustment	1. Adjust linkage
2. Improper pedal travel	2. Trim bumper stop and adjust linkage
3. Loose linkage	3. Replace as necessary
4. Faulty pilot bearing	4. Replace bearing
5. Faulty driven disc	5. Replace disc
6. Fork off ball stud	6. Install properly and lubricate fingers at throw-out bearing with wheel bearing grease.
7. Clutch disc hub binding on clutch gear spline	7. Repair or replace clutch gear and/or disc.
8. Clutch disc warp or bent	8. Replace disc (run-out should not exceed .020'').

- **PROBLEM — CLUTCH CHATTER**

Possible Cause	*Correction*
1. Worn or damaged disc assembly.	1. Replace disc assembly.
2. Grease or oil on disc facings.	2. Replace disc assembly and correct cause of contamination.
3. Improperly adjusted cover assembly.	3. Replace cover assembly.
4. Broken or loose engine mounts.	4. Replace or tighten mounts.
5. Misaligned clutch housing.	5. Align clutch housing.
6. Worn clutch gear.	6. Replace clutch gear.

• PROBLEM — CLUTCH SLIPPING

Possible Cause

1. Insufficient pedal free play.
2. Burned, worn, or oil soaked facings.
3. Weak or broken pressure springs.
4. Warped pressure plate or flywheel.
5. Driven plate not seated.

6. Driven plate over heated.

Correction

1. Adjust release fork rod.
2. Replace disc assembly and correct cause of contamination.
3. Replace cover assembly.
4. Replace pressure plate or flywheel.
5. Make 30-40 normal starts but Do Not Overheat.
6. Allow to cool and check adjustment.

• PROBLEM — DIFFICULT GEAR SHIFTING

Possible Cause

1. Excessive pedal free play.
2. Excessive deflection in linkage or firewall.
3. Worn or damaged disc assembly.
4. Improperly adjusted cover assembly.
5. Clutch disc splines sticking.

6. Worn or dry pilot bushing.
7. Clutch housing misaligned.

Correction

1. Adjust release fork rod.
2. Repair or replace linkage.

3. Replace disc assembly.
4. Replace cover assembly.

5. Remove disc assembly and free up splines or replace disc.
6. Lubricate or replace bushing.
7. Align clutch housing.

• PROBLEM — CLUTCH NOISY

Possible Cause

1. Dry clutch linkage.
2. Worn release bearing.
3. Worn disc assembly.
4. Worn release levers.
5. Worn or dry pilot bushing.
6. Dry contact-pressure plate lugs in cover.

Correction

1. Lubricate where necessary.
2. Replace release bearing.
3. Replace disc assembly.
4. Replace cover assembly.
5. Lubricate or replace bushing.
6. Lubricate very lightly.

• PROBLEM — RATTLING-TRANSMISSION CLICK

Possible Cause	*Correction*
1. Weak retracting springs.	1. Replace pressure plate.
2. Throw-out fork loose on ball stud or in bearing groove.	2. Check ball stud and retaining.
3. Oil in driven plate damper.	3. Replace driven disc.
4. Driven plate damper spring failure.	4. Replace driven disc.

• PROBLEM — THROWOUT BEARING NOISE WITH CLUTCH FULLY ENGAGED

Possible Cause	*Correction*
1. Improper adjustment.	1. Adjust linkage.
2. Throw-out bearing binding on transmission bearing retainer.	2. Clean, relubricate, check for burrs, nicks, etc.
3. Insufficient tension between clutch fork spring and ball stud.	3. Replace fork.
4. Fork improperly installed.	4. Install properly.
5. Weak linkage return spring.	5. Replace spring.

• PROBLEM — PEDAL STAYS ON FLOOR WHEN DISENGAGED

Possible Cause	*Correction*
1. Bind in linkage or release bearing.	1. Lubricate and free up linkage and release bearing.
2. Springs weak in pressure plate.	2. Replace pressure plate.
3. Springs being over traveled.	3. Adjust linkage to get proper lash, be sure proper pedal stop (bumper) is installed.

• PROBLEM — HARD PEDAL EFFORT

Possible Cause	Correction
1. Bind in linkage.	1. Lubricate and free up linkage.
2. Driven plate worn.	2. Replace driven plate.

• PROBLEM — TRANSMISSION SHIFTS HARD

Possible Cause	Correction
1. Incorrect clutch adjustment.	1. Adjust clutch pedal free-play.
2. Clutch linkage binding.	2. Lubricate or repair linkage as required.
3. Gearshift linkage incorrectly adjusted, bent, or binding.	3. Adjust linkage—correct any bind. Replace bent parts.
4. Bind in steering column, or column is misaligned.	4. Disconnect shift rods at column. Check for bind/misalignment between tube and jacket by shifting lever into all positions. Correct as required.
5. Incorrect lubricant.	5. Drain and refill transmission.
6. Internal bind in transmissions — e.g. shift rails, interlocks, shift forks, synchronizer teeth.	6. Remove transmission and inspect shift mechanism. Repair as required.
7. Clutch housing misalignment.	7. Check runout at rear face of clutch housing.

• PROBLEM — GEAR CLASH WHEN SHIFTING FROM ONE FORWARD GEAR TO ANOTHER

Possible Cause	Correction
1. Incorrect clutch adjustment.	1. Adjust clutch.
2. Clutch linkage binding.	2. Lubricate or repair linkage as required.
3. Gear shift linkage incorrectly adjusted, bent or binding.	3. Adjust linkage, correct binds, replace bent parts.
4. Clutch housing misalignment.	4. Check runout at rear face of clutch housing.

5. Damaged or worn transmission components: shift forks, synchronizers, shift rails and interlocks. Excessive end play due to worn thrust washers.

5. Inspect components. Repair or replace as required.

• PROBLEM — TRANSMISSION NOISY

Possible Cause

1. Insufficient lubricant.

2. Incorrect lubricant.
3. Clutch housing to engine or transmission to clutch housing bolts loose.
4. Dirt, chips in lubricant.
5. Gearshift linkage incorrectly adjusted, or bent or binding.
6. Clutch housing misalignment.

7. Worn transmission components: front-rear bearings, worn gear teeth, damaged gear teeth or synchronizer components.

Correction

1. Check lubricant level and replenish as required.
2. Replace with proper lubricant.
3. Check and correct bolt torque as required.

4. Drain and flush transmission.
5. Adjust linkage, correct binds, replace bent parts.
6. Check runout at rear face of clutch housing.

7. Inspect components and repair as required.

• PROBLEM — TRANSMISSION NOISY IN HIGH GEAR

Possible Cause

1. Damaged main drive gear bearing
2. Damaged mainshaft bearing
3. Damaged high speed gear synchronizer

Correction

1. Replace damaged bearing
2. Replace damaged bearing
3. Replace synchronizer

• PROBLEM — TRANSMISSION NOISY IN NEUTRAL WITH ENGINE RUNNING

Possible Cause

1. Damaged main drive gear bearing

Correction

1. Replace damaged bearing

1. Damaged or loose mainshaft pilot bearing.
2. Worn or damaged countergear anti-lash plate.
3. Worn countergear bearings.

1. Replace pilot bearings.
2. Replace countergear.
3. Replace countergear bearings and shaft.

● **PROBLEM — TRANSMISSION NOISY IN ALL REDUCTION GEARS**

Possible Cause

Correction

1. Insufficient lubricant
2. Worn or damaged main drive gear or countergear

1. Fill to correct level.
2. Replace faulty or damaged gears.

● **PROBLEM — TRANSMISSION NOISY IN SECOND ONLY**

Possible Cause

Correction

1. Damaged or worn second-speed constant mesh gears
2. Worn or damaged countergear rear bearings
3. Damaged or worn second-speed synchronizer

1. Replace damaged gears
2. Replace countergear bearings and shaft
3. Replace synchronizer

● **PROBLEM — TRANSMISSION NOISY IN THIRD ONLY (FOUR SPEED)**

Possible Cause

Correction

1. Damaged or worn third-speed constant mesh gears
2. Worn or damaged countergear bearings

1. Replace damaged gears.
2. Replace damaged countergear bearings and shaft

TDG 39

• PROBLEM — TRANSMISSION NOISY IN REVERSE ONLY

Possible Cause	*Correction*
1. Worn or damaged reverse idler gear or idler bushing.	1. Replace reverse idler gear assembly.
2. Worn or damaged reverse gear on mainshaft.	2. Replace reverse gear.
3. Damaged or worn reverse countergear.	3. Replace countergear assembly.
4. Damaged shift mechanism.	4. Inspect linkage and adjust or replace damaged parts.

• PROBLEM — EXCESSIVE BACKLASH IN ALL REDUCTION GEARS

Possible Cause	*Correction*
1. Worn countergear bearings.	1. Replace bearings.
2. Excessive end play in countergear.	2. Replace countergear thrust washers.

• PROBLEM — TRANSMISSION LEAKS

Possible Cause	*Correction*
1. Excessive amount of lubricant in transmission.	1. Drain lubricant lever
2. Loose or broken main drive gear bearing retainer.	2. Tighten or replace retainer
3. Main drive gear bearing retainer gasket damaged.	3. Replace gasket
4. Side cover loose or gasket damaged.	4. Tighten cover or replace gasket
5. Rear bearing retainer oil seal leaks.	5. Replace seal
6. Countershaft loose in case.	6. Replace case
7. Shift lever seals leak.	7. Replace seal

• PROBLEM — JUMPS OUT OF GEAR

Possible Cause	*Correction*
1. Gearshift linkage incorrectly adjusted.	1. Adjust linkage.
2. Gearshift linkage bent or binding.	2. Correct bind, replace bent parts.
3. Clutch housing misaligned.	3. Check runout at rear face of clutch housing.
4. Worn pilot bushing.	4. Replace bushings.
5. Worn or damaged clutch shaft roller bearings.	5. Replace bearings.
6. Worn, tapered gear teeth; synchronizer parts worn.	6. Inspect and replace as required.
7. Shifter forks, shift rails, or detent-interlock parts worn, missing, etc.	7. Inspect and replace as required.
8. Excessive end play of output shaft gear train, countershaft gear or reverse idler gear.	8. Replace thrust washers, and snap rings (output shaft gear train).

• PROBLEM — WILL NOT SHIFT INTO ONE GEAR—ALL OTHERS OK

Possible Cause	*Correction*
1. Gearshift linkage not adjusted correctly.	1. Adjust linkage.
2. Bent shift rod at transmission.	2. Replace rod.
3. Transmission shifter levers reversed.	3. Correctly position levers.
4. Worn or damaged shift rails, shift forks, detent-interlock plugs, loose setscrew in shifter fork, worn synchronizer parts.	4. Inspect and repair or replace parts as required.

• PROBLEM — LOCKED IN ONE GEAR—CAN NOT BE SHIFTED OUT OF THAT GEAR

Possible Cause	*Correction*
1. Gearshift linkage binding or bent.	1. Correct bind, replace bent components.
2. Transmission shifter lever attaching nuts loose or levers are worn at shifter fork shaft hole.	2. Tighten nuts, replace worn levers.

TDG 41

3. Shift rails worn or broken, shifter fork bent, setscrew loose, detent-interlock plug missing or worn.

3. Inspect and replace worn or damaged parts.

4. Broken gear teeth on countershaft gear, clutch shaft, or reverse idler gear.

4. Inspect and replace damaged part.

BRAKES

- **PROBLEM — LOW BRAKE PEDAL (Excessive pedal travel required to apply brake)**

Possible Cause

Correction

1. Excessive clearance between linings and drums caused by inoperative automatic adjusters.

1. Make 10 to 15 firm forward and reverse brake stops to adjust brakes. If brake pedal does not come up, repair or replace adjuster parts as necessary.

2. Worn brake lining.

2. Inspect and replace lining if worn beyond minimum thickness specification.

3. Bent, distorted brakeshoes.
4. Caliper pistons corroded.
5. Power unit push rod height incorrect.

3. Replace brakeshoes in axle sets.
4. Repair or replace calipers.
5. Check height with gauge (only). Replace power unit if push rod height is not within specifications.

- **PROBLEM — LOW BRAKE PEDAL (Pedal may go to floor under steady pressure)**

Possible Cause

Correction

1. Leak in hydraulic system.

1. Fill master cylinder to within ¼" of rim; have helper apply brakes and check calipers, wheel cylinders, combination valve, tubes hoses and fittings for leaks. Repair or replace parts as necessary.

2. Air in hydraulic system.

2. Bleed air from system.

3. Incorrect or non-recommended brake fluid (fluid boils away at below normal temp.).

3. Flush hydraulic system with clean brake fluid. Refill with correct-type fluid.

- **PROBLEM — LOW BRAKE PEDAL (Pedal goes to floor on first application—Ok on subsequent applications)**

Possible Cause

Correction

1. Disc brakeshoe (pad) knock back; shoes push caliper piston back into bore. Caused by loose wheel bearings or excessive lateral run-out of rotor (rotor wobble).

1. Adjust wheel bearings and check lateral runout of rotor(s). Refinish rotors if runout is over limits. Replace rotor if refinishing would cause rotor to fall below minimum thickness limit.

2. Calipers sticking on mounting surfaces of caliper and anchor. Caused by buildup of dirt, rust, or corrosion on abutment.

2. Clean mounting surfaces and lubricate surfaces with molydisulphide grease or equivalent.

- **PROBLEM — FADING BRAKE PEDAL (Pedal falls away under steady pressure)**

Possible Cause

Correction

1. Leak in hydraulic system.

1. Fill master cylinder reservoirs to within ¼″ of rim; have helper apply brakes check master cylinder, calipers, wheel cylinders combination valve, tubes, hoses, and fittings for leaks. Repair or replace parts as necessary.

2. Master cylinder piston cups worn, or master cylinder bore is scored, worn or corroded.

2. Repair or replace master cylinder.

- **PROBLEM — DECREASING BRAKE PEDAL, TRAVEL (Pedal travel required to apply brakes decreases, may be accompanied by hard pedal)**

Possible Cause	*Correction*
1. Caliper or wheel cylinder pistons sticking or seized.	1. Repair or replace calipers, or wheel cylinders.
2. Master cylinder compensator ports blocked (preventing fluid return to reservoirs) or pistons sticking or seized in master cylinder bore.	2. Repair or replace master cylinder.
3. Power brake unit binding internally.	3. Test unit as follows:
	(a) Raise hood, shift transmission into neutral and start engine.
	(b) Increase engine speed to 1500 RPM, close throttle and fully depress brake pedal.
	(c) Slowly release brake pedal and stop engine.
	(d) Remove vacuum check valve and hose from power unit. Observe for backward movement of brake pedal or power unit-to-brake pedal push rod.
	(e) If pedal or push rod move backward, power unit has internal bind—replace power brake unit.
4. Incorrect power unit push rod height.	4. Adjust push rod height.

- **PROBLEM — SPONGY BRAKE PEDAL (Pedal has abnormally soft, springy, spongy feel when depressed)**

Possible Cause

1. Air in hydraulic system.
2. Brake shoes bent or distorted.
3. Brake lining not yet seated to drums and rotors.

Correction

1. Bleed brakes.
2. Replace brakeshoes.
3. Burnish brakes.

- **PROBLEM — HARD BRAKE PEDAL (Excessive pedal pressure required to stop car. May be accompanied by brake fade)**

Possible Cause

1. Loose or leaking power brake unit vacuum hose.
2. Brake lining contaminated by grease or brake fluid.

3. Incorrect or poor quality brake lining.
4. Bent, broken, distorted brakeshoes.
5. Calipers binding or dragging on anchor. Rear brakeshoes dragging on support plate.

6. Rear brake drum(s) bell mouthed (flared or barrel shaped (distorted).
7. Caliper, wheel cylinder, or master cylinder pistons sticking or seized.

Correction

1. Tighten connections or replace leaking hose.
2. Determine cause of contaminations and correct. Replace contaminated brake lining in axle sets.
3. Replace lining in axle sets.
4. Replace brakeshoes and lining.
5. Sand or wire brush anchors and caliper mounting surfaces and lubricate surfaces lightly. Clean rust or burrs from rear brake support plate ledges and lubricate ledges. **NOTE:** If ledges are deeply grooved or scored, do not attempt to sand or grind them smooth—replace support plate.
6. Replace rear drum(s).
7. Repair or replace parts as necessary.

8. Power brake unit vacuum check valve malfunction.

8. Test valve as follows:
   (a) Start engine, increase engine speed to 1500 RPM, close throttle and immediately stop engine.
   (b) Wait at least 90 seconds then try brake action.
   (c) If brakes are not vacuum assisted for 2 or more applications, check valve is faulty.

9. Power brake unit has internal bind or incorrect push rod height (too long).

9. Test unit as follows:
   (a) With engine stopped, apply brakes several times to exhaust all vacuum in system.
   (b) Shift transmission into neutral, depress brake pedal and start engine.
   (c) If pedal falls away under foot pressure and less pressure is required to hold pedal in applied position, power unit vacuum system is working. Test power unit as outlined in item (3) under Decreasing Brake Pedal Travel. If power unit exhibits bind condition, replace power unit.
   (d) If power unit does not exhibit bind condition, disconnect master cylinder and check push rod height with appropriate gauge. If height is not within specifications, replace power unit.

10. Master cylinder compensator ports (at bottom of reservoirs) blocked by dirt, scale, rust, or have small burrs (blocked ports prevent fluid return to reservoirs).

10. Repair or replace master cylinder. **CAUTION:** Do not attempt to clean blocked ports with wire, pencils, or similar implements.

11. Brake hoses, tubes, fittings clogged or restricted.

11. Use compressed air to check or unclog parts. Replace any damaged parts.

12. Brake fluid contaminated with improper fluids (motor oil, transmission fluid, or poor quality brake fluid) causing rubber components to swell and stick in bores.	12. Replace all rubber components and hoses. Flush entire brake system. Refill with recommended brake fluid.

● **PROBLEM — GRABBING BRAKES (Severe reaction to brake pedal pressure)**

Possible Cause	*Correction*
1. Brake lining(s) contaminated by grease or brake fluid.	1. Determine and correct cause of contamination and replace brakeshoes and linings in axle sets.
2. Parking brake cables incorrectly adjusted or seized.	2. Adjust cables. Free up or replace seized cables.
3. Power brake unit binding internally or push rod height incorrect.	3. Test unit as outlined in item (3) under Decreasing Brake Pedal Travel. If o.k., check push rod height. If unit has internal bind or incorrect push rod height, replace unit.
4. Incorrect brake lining or lining loose on brakeshoes.	4. Replace brakeshoes in axle sets.
5. Brakeshoes bent, cracked, distorted.	5. Replace brakeshoes in axle sets.
6. Caliper anchor plate bolts loose.	6. Tighten bolts.
7. Rear brakeshoes binding on support plate ledges.	7. Clean and lubricate ledges. Replace support plate(s) if ledges are deeply grooved. Do not attempt to smooth ledges by grinding.
8. Rear brake support plate loose.	8. Tighten mounting bolts.
9. Caliper or wheel cylinder piston sticking or seized.	9. Repair or replace parts as necessary.
10. Master cylinder pistons sticking or seized in bore.	10. Repair or replace master cylinder.

- **PROBLEM — BRAKES GRAB, PULL, OR WON'T HOLD IN WET WEATHER**

Possible Cause	*Correction*
1. Brake lining water soaked.	1. Drive car with brakes lightly applied to dry out lining. If problem persists after lining has dried, replace brakeshoe lining in axle sets.
2. Rear brake support plate bent allowing excessive amount of water to enter drum.	2. Replace support plate.

- **PROBLEM — DRAGGING BRAKES (Slow or incomplete release of brakes)**

Possible Cause	*Correction*
1. Brake pedal binding at pivot.	1. Free up and lubricate.
2. Power brake unit push rod height incorrect (too high) or unit has internal bind.	2. Replace unit if push rod height is incorrect. If height is o.k., check for internal bind as outlined in item (3) under Decreasing Brake Pedal Travel.
3. Parking brake cables incorrectly adjusted or seized.	3. Adjust cables. Free up or replace seized cables.
4. Brakeshoe return springs weak or broken.	4. Replace return springs. Replace brake shoe if necessary in axle sets.
5. Automatic adjusters malfunctioning.	5. Repair or replace adjuster parts as required.
6. Caliper, wheel cylinder or master cylinder pistons sticking or seized.	6. Repair or replace parts as necessary.
7. Master cylinder compensating ports blocked (fluid does not return to reservoirs).	7. Use compressed air to clear ports. Do not use wire, pencils, or similar objects to open blocked ports.

- ## PROBLEM — CAR PULLS TO ONE SIDE WHEN BRAKES ARE APPLIED

Possible Cause	*Correction*
1. Incorrect front tire pressure.	1. Inflate to recommended cold (reduced load) inflation pressure.
2. Incorrect front wheel bearing adjustment or worn—damaged wheel bearings.	2. Adjust wheel bearings. Replace worn, damaged bearings.
3. Brakeshoe lining on one side contaminated.	3. Determine and correct cause of contamination and replace brakeshoe lining in axle sets.
4. Brakeshoes on one side bent, distorted, or lining loose on shoe.	4. Replace brakeshoes in axle sets.
5. Support plate bent or loose on one side.	5. Tighten or replace support plate.
6. Brake lining not yet seated to drums and rotors.	6. Burnish brakes.
7. Caliper anchor plate loose on one side.	7. Tighten anchor plate bolts.
8. Caliper or wheel cylinder piston sticking or seized.	8. Repair or replace caliper or wheel cylinder.
9. Brake shoe linings watersoaked.	9. Drive car with brakes lightly applied to dry linings. Replace brakeshoes in axle sets if problem persists.
10. Loose suspension component attaching or mounting bolts, incorrect front end alignment. Worn suspension parts.	10. Tighten suspension bolts. Replace worn suspension components. Check and correct alignment as necessary.

- ## PROBLEM — CHATTER OR SHUDDER WHEN BRAKES ARE APPLIED (Pedal pulsation and roughness may also occur)

Possible Cause	*Correction*
1. Front wheel bearings loose.	1. Adjust wheel bearings.
2. Brake shoes distorted, bent, contaminated, or worn.	2. Replace brakeshoes in axle sets.

3. Caliper anchor plate or support plate loose.

3. Tighten mounting bolts.

4. Excessive thickness variation or lateral rim out of rotor.

4. Refinish or replace rotor.

5. Rear drum(s) out of round, sharp spots.

5. Refinish or replace drum.

6. Loose suspension component attaching or mounting bolts, incorrect front end alignment. Worn suspension parts.

6. Tighten suspension bolts. Replace worn suspension components. Check and correct alignment as necessary.

● **PROBLEM — NOISY BRAKES (Squealing, clicking, scraping sound when brakes are applied**

Possible Cause

Correction

1. Bent, broken, distorted brakeshoes.

1. Replace brakeshoes in axle sets.

2. Brake lining worn out—shoes contacting drum or rotor.

2. Replace brakeshoes and lining in axle sets. Refinish or replace drums or rotors.

3. Foreign material imbedded in brake lining.

3. Replace brake lining.

4. Broken or loose holdown or return springs.

4. Replace parts as necessary.

5. Rough or dry drum brake support plate ledges.

5. Lubricate support plate ledges.

6. Cracked, grooved or scored rotor(s) or drum(s).

6. Replace rotor(s) or drum(s). Replace brakeshoes and lining in axle sets if necessary.

● **PROBLEM — PULSATING BRAKE PEDAL**

Possible Cause

Correction

1. Out of round drums or excessive thickness variation or lateral runout in disc brake rotor(s).

1. Refinish or replace drums or rotors.

2. Bent rear axle shaft.

2. Replace axle shaft.

TDG 50

SUSPENSION & STEERING

• PROBLEM — HARD OR ERRATIC STEERING

Possible Cause	*Correction*
1. Incorrect tire pressure.	1. Inflate tires to recommended pressures.
2. Insufficient or incorrect lubrication.	2. Lubricate as required.
3. Suspension, steering or linkage parts damaged or misaligned.	3. Repair or replace parts as necessary.
4. Improper front wheel alignment.	4. Adjust wheel alignment angles.
5. Incorrect steering gear adjustment.	5. Adjust steering gear.
6. Sagging springs.	6. Replace springs.

• PROBLEM — PLAY OR LOOSENESS IN STEERING

Possible Cause	*Correction*
1. Steering wheel loose.	1. Inspect splines and repair as necessary. Tighten steering wheel nut.
2. Steering linkage or attaching parts loose or worn.	2. Tighten, adjust, or replace faulty components.
3. Pitman arm loose.	3. Inspect shaft splines and repair as necessary. Torque attaching nut and stake in place.
4. Steering gear attaching bolts loose.	4. Tighten bolts.
5. Loose or worn wheel bearings.	5. Adjust or replace bearings.
6. Steering gear adjustment incorrect or parts badly worn.	6. Adjust gear or replace defective parts.

• PROBLEM — WHEEL SHIMMY OR TRAMP

Possible Cause	*Correction*
1. Improper tire pressure.	1. Inflate tires to recommended pressures.
2. Wheels, tires, or brake drums out-of-balance or out-of-round.	2. Inspect parts and replace unacceptable out-of-round parts. Rebalance parts.

3. Inoperative, worn, or loose shock absorbers or mounting parts.
4. Loose or worn steering or suspension parts.
5. Loose or worn wheel bearings.
6. Incorrect steering gear adjustments.
7. Incorrect front wheel alignment.

3. Repair or replace shocks or mountings.
4. Tighten or replace as necessary.
5. Adjust or replace bearings.
6. Adjust steering gear.
7. Correct front wheel alignment.

- **PROBLEM — CAR LEADS TO ONE SIDE**

Possible Cause

Correction

1. Improper tire pressures.

2. Front tires with uneven tread depth, wear pattern or different cord design (i.e., one bias play and one belted tire on front wheels).
3. Incorrect front wheel alignment.
4. Brakes dragging.
5. Faulty power steering gear valve assembly.
6. Pulling due to uneven tire construction.

1. Inflate tires to recommended pressures.

2. Install tires of same cord construction and reasonably even tread depth and wear pattern.

3. Align incorrect angles.
4. Adjust or repair brakes.
5. Replace valve assembly.

6. Replace faulty tire.

- **PROBLEM — POOR DIRECTIONAL STABILITY**

Possible Cause

Correction

1. Ball joints and steering linkage need lubrication.
2. Low or uneven front or rear tire pressure.
3. Loose wheel bearings.
4. Steering gear not on high point.
5. Incorrect front wheel alignment (caster).
6. Broken springs.
7. Malfunctioning shock absorber.
8. Broken stabilizer bar, or missing link

1. Lubricate at proper intervals.

2. Inflate tires to the proper recommended pressure.

3. Adjust wheel bearings.
4. Adjust steering gear.
5. Check and align front suspension.

6. Replace springs
7. Diagnose shock abosrbers.
8. Replace stabilizer or link.

• PROBLEM — VEHICLE PULLS TO ONE SIDE, BRAKES NOT APPLIED

Possible Cause	*Correction*
1. Low or uneven tire pressure.	1. Inflate tires to the proper recommended pressure.
2. Front or rear brake dragging.	2. Adjust brakes.
3. Broken or sagging front spring.	3. Replace spring.
4. Incorrect front wheel alignment (Camber).	4. Check and align front suspension.

• PROBLEM — "DOG" TRACKING

Possible Cause   *Correction*

LEAF TYPE REAR SPRING

1. Rear leaf spring broken.	1. Replace spring.
2. Bent rear axle housing.	2. Replace housing.
3. Frame or underbody out of alignment.	3. Align frame.

COIL TYPE REAR SPRING

1. Damage rear suspension arm and/or worn bushings.	1. Replace suspension arm and/bushings.
2. Frame out of alignment.	2. Align frame.
3. Bent rear axle housing.	3. Replace housing.

• PROBLEM — RETURNABILITY POOR

Possible Cause	*Correction*
1. Steering linkage needs lubrication.	1. Lubricate chassis.
2. Idler arm bushing worn.	2. Replace idler arm.
3. Steering gear adjustment.	3. Adjust gear.
4. Improper caster setting (negative).	4. Check and reset if necessary.

- ### PROBLEM — ERRATIC STEERING ON BRAKE APPLICATION

Possible Cause	*Correction*
1. Low or uneven tire pressure.	1. Inflate tires to proper recommended pressure.
2. Front wheel bearing incorrectly adjusted.	2. Adjust bearing as necessary.
3. Brakes incorrectly or unevenly adjusted.	3. Adjust brakes as necessary.
4. Front spring sagged.	4. Replace spring if necessary.
5. Steering gear off high point.	5. Check and correct steering if necessary.
6. Incorrect or uneven caster.	6. Check and adjust caster as necessary.
7. Leaking wheel cylinders.	7. Replace

- ### PROBLEM — NOISE IN FRONT END

Possible Cause	*Correction*
1. Ball joints and steering linkage need lubrication.	1. Lubricate at recommended intervals.
2. Shock absorber loose or bushings worn.	2. Tighten bolts and/or replace bushings.
3. Worm control arm bushings.	3. Replace bushings.
4. Worn tie rod ends.	4. Replace tie rod ends.
5. Worn or loose wheel bearings.	5. Adjust or replace wheel bearings.
6. Loose stabilizer bar.	6. Tighten all stabilizer bar attachments.
7. Loose wheel nuts.	7. Tighten the wheel nuts to proper torque.
8. Spring improperly positioned.	8. Reposition.
9. Loose suspension bolts.	9. Torque to specifications or replace.

- ### PROBLEM — WHEEL TRAMP

Possible Cause	*Correction*
1. Tire and wheel out of balance.	1. Balance wheels.
2. Tire and wheel out of round.	2. Replace tire.
3. Blister or bump on tire.	3. Replace tire.
4. Improper shock absorber action.	4. Replace shock absorber.

• PROBLEM — TIRE WEAR

Possible Cause   *Correction*

1. Improper tire pressure.
2. Failure to rotate tires.
3. Brakes grabbing.
4. Incorrect front wheel alignment.
5. Broken or damaged steering and suspension parts.
6. Wheel runout.
7. Excessive speed on turns.

1. Inflate tires to recommended pressures.
2. Rotate tires.
3. Adjust or repair brakes.
4. Align incorrect angles.
5. Repair or replace defective parts.

6. Replace faulty wheel.
7. Make driver aware of condition.

• PROBLEM — EXCESSIVE OR UNEVEN TIRE WEAR

Possible Cause   *Correction*

1. Underinflated or overinflated tires.
2. Improper toe-in.
3. Wheels out of balance.
4. Hard driving.
5. Over loaded vehicle.

1. Inflate tire to proper recommended pressure.
2. Adjust toe-in.
3. Balance wheels.
4. Instruct driver.
5. Instruct driver.

• PROBLEM — SCUFFED TIRES

Possible Cause   *Correction*

1. Toe-in incorrect.
2. Excessive speed on turns.
3. Tires improperly inflated.

4. Suspension arm bent or twisted.

1. Adjust toe-in to specifications.
2. Advise driver.
3. Inflate tires to proper recommended pressure.
4. Replace arm.

• PROBLEM — CUPPED TIRES

Possible Cause   *Correction*

1. Front shock absorbers defective.   1. Replace shock absorbers.
2. Worn ball joints.   2. Replace ball joints.
3. Wheel bearings incorrectly ad-   3. Adjust or replace wheel bearings.
   justed or worn.
4. Wheel and tire out of balance.   4. Balance wheel and tire.
5. Excessive tire or wheel runout.   5. Compensate for runout.

HEADLAMPS

• PROBLEM — ONE HEADLAMP INOPERATIVE OR INTERMITTENT

Possible Cause   *Correction*

1. Loose connection.   1. Secure connections to sealed
                                                         beam including ground.
2. Defective sealed beam.   2. Replace sealed beam.

• PROBLEM — ONE OR MORE HEADLIGHTS ARE DIM

Possible Cause   *Correction*

1. Open ground connection at head-   1. Repair ground wire connection
   light.   between sealed beam and body
                                                         ground.
2. Ground wire mislocated in head-   2. Relocate ground wire in connec-
   light connector (type 2 sealed   tor.
   beam).

• PROBLEM — ONE OR MORE HEADLIGHTS SHORT LIFE

Possible Cause   *Correction*

1. Voltage regulator maladjusted.   1. Readjust   regulator   to
                                                         specifications.

• PROBLEM — ALL HEADLIGHTS INOPERATIVE OR INTERMITTENT

Possible Cause   *Correction*

1. Loose connection.   1. Check and secure connections at
                                                         dimmer switch and light switch.

2. Defective dimmer switch.

2. Check voltage at dimmer switch with test lamp. If test lamp bulb lights only at switch "Hot" wire terminal, replace dimmer switch..

3. Open wiring — light switch to dimmer switch.

3. Check wiring with test lamp. If bulb lights at light switch wire terminal, but not at dimmer switch, repair open wire.

4. Open wiring — light switch to battery.

4. Check "Hot" wire terminal at light switch with test lamp. If lamp does not light, repair open wire circuit to battery (possible open fusible link).

5. Shorted ground circuit.

5. If, after a few minutes operation, headlights flicker "ON" and "OFF" and/or a thumping noise can be heard from the light switch (circuit breaker opening and closing), repair short to ground in circuit between light switch and headlights. After repairing short, check for headlight flickering after one minute of operation. If flickering occurs, the circuit breaker has been damaged and light switch must be replaced.

6. Defective light switch.

6. Check light switch. Replace light switch, if defective.

- **PROBLEM — UPPER OR LOWER BEAM WILL NOT LIGHT OR INTERMITTENT**

Possible Cause

Correction

1. Open connection or defective dimmer switch.

1. Check dimmer switch terminals with test lamps. If bulb lights at all wire terminals, repair open wiring between dimmer switch and headlights. If bulb will not light at one of these terminals, replace dimmer switch.

2. Short circuit to ground.

2. Follow diagnosis above (all headlights inoperative or intermittent).

TDG 57

SIDE MARKER LAMPS

• PROBLEM — ONE LAMP INOPERATIVE

Possible Cause

1. Turn signal bulb burnt out (front lamp).
2. Side marker bulb burned out.
3. Loose connection or open in wiring.

Correction

1. Switch turn signals on. If signal bulb does not light, replace bulb.
2. Replace bulb.
3. Using test lamp, check "Hot" wire terminal at bulb socket. If test lamp lights, repair open ground circuit. If lamp does not light, repair open "Hot" wire circuit.

• PROBLEM — FRONT OR REAR LAMPS INOPERATIVE

Possible Cause

1. Loose connection or open ground connection.

2. Multiple bulbs burnt out.

Correction

1. If associated tail or park lamps do not operate, secure all connectors in "Hot" wire circuit. If park and turn lamps operate, repair open ground connections.
2. Replace burnt out bulbs.

• PROBLEM — ALL LAMPS INOPERATIVE

Possible Cause

1. Blown fuse.

2. Loose connection.
3. Open in wiring.

Correction

1. If park and tail lamps do not operate, replace blown fuse. If new fuse blows, check for short to ground between fuse panel and lamps.
2. Secure connector to light switch.
3. Check tail light fuse with test lamp. If test lamp lights, repair open wiring between fuse and light switch. If not, repair open wiring between fuse and battery (possible open fusible link).

4. Defective light switch.

4. Check light switch. Replace light switch, if defective.

TAIL, PARK AND LICENSE LAMPS

● PROBLEM — ONE SIDE INOPERATIVE

Possible Cause

Correction

1. Bulb burnt out.
2. Open ground connection at bulb socket or ground wire terminal.

1. Replace bulb.
2. Jumper bulb base socket connection to ground. If lamp lights, repair open ground circuit.

● PROBLEM — BOTH SIDES INOPERATIVE

Possible Cause

Correction

1. Tail lamp fuse blown.

1. Replace fuse. If new fuse blows, repair short to ground in "Hot" wire circuit between fuse panel through light switch to lamps.

2. Loose connection.
3. Open wiring.

2. Secure connector at light switch.
3. Using test light, check circuit on both sides of fuse. If lamp does not light on either side, repair open circuit between fuse panel and pattery (possible open fusible link). If test lamp lights at light switch terminal, repair open wiring between light switch and lamps.

4. Multiple bulb burnout.

4. If test lamp lights at lamp socket "Hot" wire terminal, replace bulbs.

5. Defective light switch.

5. Check light switch. Replace light switch, if defective.

TURN SIGNAL AND HAZARD WARNING LAMP

• PROBLEM — TURN SIGNALS INOPERATIVE ONE SIDE

Possible Cause	*Correction*
1. Bulb(s) burnt out (flasher cannot be heard).	1. Turn hazard warning system on. If one or more bulbs are inoperative replace necessary bulbs.
2. Open wiring or ground connection.	2. Turn hazard warning system on. If one or more bulbs are inoperative, use test lamp and check circuit at lamp socket. If test lamp lights, repair open ground connection. If not, repair open wiring between bulb socket and turn signal switch.
3. Improper bulb or defective turn signal switch.	3. Turn hazard warning system on. If all front and rear lamps operate, check for improper bulb. If bulbs are OK, replace defective turn signal switch.
4. Short to ground (flasher can be heard, no bulbs operate).	4. Locate and repair short to ground by disconnecting front and rear circuits separately.

• PROBLEM — TURN SIGNALS INOPERATIVE

Possible Cause	*Correction*
1. Blown turn signal fuse.	1. Turn hazard warning system on. If all lamps operate, replace blown fuse. If new fuse blows, repair short to ground between fuse and lamps.
2. Defective flasher.	2. If turn signal fuse is OK and hazard warning system will operate lamps, replace defective turn signal flasher.
3. Loose connection.	3. Secure steering column connector.

- ## PROBLEM — HAZARD WARNING LAMPS INOPERATIVE

Possible Cause	*Correction*
1. Blown fuse.	1. Switch turn signals on. If lamps operate, replace fuse if blown. If new fuse blows, repair short to ground (could be in stop light circuit).
2. Defective hazard warning flasher.	2. If fuse is OK, switch turn signals on. If lamps operate, replace defective hazard flahser.
3. Open in wiring or defective turn signal switch.	3. Using test lamp, check hazard switch feed wire in turn signal steering column connector. If lamp does not light on either side of connector, repair open circuit between flasher and connector. If lamp lights only on feed side of connector, clean connector contacts. If lamp lights on both sides of connector, replace defective turn signal switch assembly.

BACK-UP LAMP

- ## PROBLEM — ONE LAMP INOPERATIVE OR INTERMITTENT

Possible Cause	*Correction*
1. Loose or burnt out bulb.	1. Secure or replace bulb.
2. Loose connection.	2. Tighten connectors.
3. Open ground connections.	3. Repair bulb ground circuit.

- ## PROBLEM — BOTH LAMPS INOPERATIVE OR INTERMITTENT

Possible Cause	*Correction*
1. Neutral start or back-up lamp switch maladjusted.	1. Readjust neutral start or back-up lamp switch.

2. Loose connection or open circuit.	2. Secure all connectors. If OK, check continuity of circuit from fuse to lamps with test lamp. If lamp does not light on either side of fuse, correct open circuit from battery to fuse.
3. Blown fuse.	3. Replace fuse. If new fuse blows, repair short to ground in circuit from fuse through neutral start switch to back-up lamps.
4. Defective neutral start or back-up lamp switch.	4. Check switch. Replace neutral start or back-up lamp switch, if defective.
5. Defective ignition switch.	5. If test lamp lights at ignition switch battery terminal but not at output terminal, replace ignition switch.

• PROBLEM — LAMP WILL NOT TURN OFF

Possible Cause — *Correction*

1. Neutral start or back-up switch maladjusted.	1. Readjust neutral start or back-up lamp switch.
2. Defective neutral start or back-up lamp switch.	2. Check switch. Replace neutral start or back-up lamp switch, if defective.

STOP LIGHTS

• PROBLEM — ONE BULB INOPERATIVE

Possible Cause — *Correction*

1. Bulb burnt out.	1. Replace bulb.

• PROBLEM — ONE SIDE INOPERATIVE

Possible Cause   *Correction*

1. Loose connection, open wiring or defective bulbs.

2. Defective directional signal switch or cancelling cam.

1. Turn on directional signal. If lamp does not operate, check bulbs. If bulbs are OK, secure all connections. If lamp still does not operate, use test lamp and check for open wiring.

2. If lamp will operate by turning directional signal on, the switch is not centering properly during cancelling operation. Replace defective cancelling cam or directional signal switch.

• PROBLEM — ALL INOPERATIVE

Possible Cause   *Correction*

1. Blown fuse.

2. Stop switch maladjusted or defective.

1. Replace fuse. If new fuse blows, repair short to ground in circuit between fuse and lamps.

2. Check stop switch. Adjust or replace stop switch, if required.

• PROBLEM — WILL NOT TURN OFF

Possible Cause   *Correction*

1. Stop switch maladjusted or defective.

1. Readjust switch. If switch still malfunctions, replace.

TDG 63

HORNS

• PROBLEM — HORNS WILL NOT OPERATE

Possible Cause   *Correction*

1. Loose connections in circuit.   1. Check and tighten connections. Be sure to check ground straps.

2. Defective horn switch.   2. Replace defective parts.
3. Defective horn relay.   3. Replace relay.
4. Defects within horn.   4. Replace horn.

• PROBLEM — HORNS HAVE POOR TONE

Possible Cause   *Correction*

1. Low available voltage at horn, or defects within horn.   1. Check battery and charging circuit. Although horn should blow at any voltage above 7.0 volts, a weak or poor tone may occur at operating voltages below 11.0 volts. If horn has weak or poor tone at operating voltage of 11.0 volts or higher, remove horn and replace.

• PROBLEM — HORNS OPERATE INTERMITTENTLY

Possible Cause   *Correction*

1. Loose or intermittent connections in horn relay or horn circuit.   1. Check and tighten connections.

2. Defective horn switch.   2. Replace switch.
3. Defective relay.   3. Replace relay.
4. Defects within horn.   4. Replace horn.

• PROBLEM — HORNS BLOW CONSTANTLY

Possible Cause   *Correction*

1. Sticking horn relay.   1. Replace relay.
2. Horn relay energized by grounded or shorted wiring.   2. Check and adjust wiring.

3. Horn button can be grounded by sticking closed.   3. Adjust or replace damaged parts.